COMPETENT TO MINISTER

W9-BUP-903

The Biblical Care of Souls

Martin & Deidre Bobgan

EastGate Publishers
Santa Barbara, CA 93110

Scripture quotations are taken from the Authorized King
James Version of the Holy Bible.

For a sample copy of a free newsletter
about the intrusion of psychological
counseling theories and therapies into
the church, please write to:

PsychoHeresy Awareness Ministries
4137 Primavera Road
Santa Barbara, CA 93110

COMPETENT TO MINISTER:
THE BIBLICAL CARE OF SOULS

Copyright © 1996 Martin and Deidre Bobgan
Published by EastGate Publishers
Santa Barbara, California

Library of Congress Catalog Card Number 96-86500
ISBN 0-941717-11-9

Printed in the United States of America

For ye see your calling, brethren, how that not many wise men after the flesh, not many mighty, not many noble, are called:

But God hath chosen the foolish things of the world to confound the wise; and God hath chosen the weak things of the world to confound the things which are mighty;

And base things of the world, and things which are despised, hath God chosen, yea, and things which are not, to bring to nought things that are:

That no flesh should glory in his presence.

But of him are ye in Christ Jesus, who of God is made unto us wisdom, and righteousness, and sanctification, and redemption:

That, according as it is written, He that glorieth, let him glory in the Lord (1 Corinthians 1:26-31).

CONTENTS

1

The Biblical Care of Souls in the Body of Christ

We have been on a journey since writing our first book, *The Psychological Way/The Spiritual Way*.[1] We have written a number of books along the way, but as we were writing *Against Biblical Counseling: For the Bible*, we found it necessary to tell Moody Press that we could no longer support our book *How to Counsel from Scripture*,[2] because we had departed from the biblical counseling movement and were voicing our concerns. While *How to Counsel from Scripture* contains much material we still uphold, some of it supported the biblical counseling movement from which we had departed. Moody Press kindly put the book out of print. This current book, *Competent to Minister: The Biblical Care of Souls*, is a natural result of having departed from the biblical counseling movement and includes many of the

biblical reasons why we did. Here we encourage the
church to return to its biblical roots.

The Reformation was a turning point in church history. Two great teachings of the Reformation are *Sola
Scriptura* and the priesthood of all believers. *Sola
Scriptura* means by Scripture alone. The *priesthood of
all believers* means that believers, guided by the Word
and empowered by the Holy Spirit, are equipped and
called to minister to one another in the Body of Christ.
This book rests heavily on those two doctrines. It is a
call forward to confidence in the efficacy of Scriptures
and the knowledge that:

> All scripture is given by inspiration of God, and is
> profitable for doctrine, for reproof, for correction,
> for instruction in righteousness: That the man of
> God may be perfect, thoroughly furnished unto all
> good works (2 Timothy 3:16,17).

This book is also a call to believers to use the Word
empowered by the Spirit to minister to one another.
**You who are Christians are competent to minister
by the grace of God; you can care for souls.**

The care of souls depends upon all of the "alones" of
the Reformation:

Sola Scriptura	by Scripture alone
Sola Gratia	by grace alone
Solo Christo	by Christ alone
Sola Fide	by faith alone
Soli Deo Gloria	glory to God alone

These principles apply to all aspects of salvation,
including justification, sanctification, and glorification.
Believers are to continue their walk with the Lord on
the same basis as their initial salvation by Scripture
alone, by grace alone, by Christ alone, by faith alone,
and to the glory of God alone. All these apply within the
individual life of the believer and within the Body of
Christ, in which we have the fellowship and the priesthood of all believers.

Mutual care within the Body of Christ, performed by a priesthood of all believers also depends upon these same principles. We want to emphasize this at the very beginning because of the tenacious tendency to use other means for living the Christian life and solving problems of living. Psychological counseling violates these biblical principles. Theories and methodologies underlying psychotherapy have come from the wisdom of men and cannot be integrated with Scripture without doing violence to the Word of God. Psychological counseling depends on the works of the flesh rather than the grace of God, even when practiced by Christians. Thereby the flesh is strengthened and spiritual growth may be retarded or stagnated.

Psychological counseling is not by Christ alone, even if the counselor is a Christian, because the models and methods are unsanctified human means and depend upon unsanctified human effort. Psychological counseling depends on a faith other than faith in the Word of God and the work of the Holy Spirit. Psychological counseling depends on faith in the counselor and the counseling process. Finally, psychological counseling cannot be *Soli Deo Gloria*, because the psychology together with the counselor and the so-called counselee get the credit. Even when some credit is given to God because of a "counselor" or "counselee" being a Christian, the glory is not glory to God alone.

Much of what is called "biblical counseling" fails to support these solid biblical principles as well. About 25 years ago Dr. Jay Adams wrote a book titled *Competent to Counsel*. His book marked the beginning of what is now known as the biblical counseling movement. While Adams was attempting to encourage pastors to minister biblically, rather than psychologically, he solidified the idea of counseling as a process for Christians. Now, after years of involvement in the biblical counseling movement, we realize it was a mistake for him to call it "counseling" in the first place. What should go on between believers in the mutual care of souls would better be called "ministry," "personal ministry," "care of souls"—anything but "counseling." Why? If the process of mutual care and personal ministry of the Word of God had been called "ministry" rather than "counseling," many of the unbiblical aspects of the biblical counseling movement (such as charging fees) may never have been incorporated by those who wanted to minister biblically. Can you imagine anyone charging for ministry? Would any Christian even think of charging a fellow believer for extending mutual care in the Body of Christ? But, call it "counseling" with "counselors" and "counselees," and no one questions the required fee, because that's exactly what happens in the world. Professional "counselors" charge fees for "counseling" their "counselees."

The words *counseling* and *counselor* have become powerful symbols that place too much emphasis on the process (methodology) and the person conducting the process ("expert"). Even when Christians use the words *counsel* (**verb form**), *counselor*, *counselee*, and *counseling*, the terms are bound to meanings, expectations, and procedures of psychotherapy. Because of the psychological baggage of such words, Christians should try to avoid using them in reference to biblical ministry, even when referring to personal ministry involving those seeking wisdom and those attempting to help through listening and speaking. Possible changes are:

to counsel: to minister, evangelize, teach, pastor, disciple, come alongside, advise, give godly wisdom, encourage, admonish, exhort, edify, equip, nurture, assist another to find help in God's Word

counselor: minister, evangelist, teacher, pastor, fellow believer, elder, sister, brother, biblical care giver

counselee: fellow believer, sister, brother, (or if not a believer, possible convert), person, individual, one seeking help

> *counseling*: ministering, pastoring, evangelizing, teaching, discipling, encouraging, exhorting, admonishing, advising, edifying, equipping, nurturing, coming alongside, giving wisdom, helping another find help in God's Word

Just attempting to use different words may help believers move away from the ways of the world and towards biblically caring for souls. We would continue using the noun *counsel* in reference to godly counsel, because it is a biblical term. We encourage biblical counsel to be given through and under the ministries of the church and through mutual care in the Body of Christ. While the word *counsellor* is in Scripture, the word has been too corrupted by the psychological way to be used in reference to humans. We do continue, however, to use the word *Counselor* in reference to God.

Regardless of the original intent of Adams' book, the biblical counseling movement has evolved from its beginnings in *Competent to Counsel* to a reflection of the very psychological counseling movement it opposed. We were part of the biblical counseling movement for many years, but finally concluded that an emphasis on biblical counseling is not the solution. In a prior book we itemized our concerns with the biblical counseling movement and enumerated the errors of its ways. In this book we give a glimpse of the care of souls and an encouragement that believers ARE competent to minister to one another in the Body of Christ.

For nearly 30 years we have been questioning the use of psychological counseling (psychotherapy and its underlying psychologies) and urging Christians to return to the Bible. We used both biblical and research documentation to reveal psychology's intrinsic conflict with Scripture and its inherent weaknesses regarding usefulness. Nevertheless, multitudes of Christians view psychology with respect and awe. Even though secular psychological researchers are demonstrating less and less confidence in psychological counseling, more and more Christians are pursuing it either as therapists themselves or as clients seeking treatment. What is often referred to as "Christian psychology" or "Christian counseling" ends up being secular psychology adapted for the Christian market. Christians who are not directly involved in counseling look to what psychologists say about how to live, how to relate to others, and how to meet the challenges of life.

The Care of Souls from Pentecost Onward

In view of how many Christians have placed their faith in psychology, we often ask, "What did the church do for almost 2000 years without the psychological counseling movement?" The very first Christians ministered to those suffering from problems of living. They preached the Gospel, taught new believers, and cared for their souls. Rather than basing their ministry on psychological theories, they based their ministry on what Jesus had taught them and also on the Scriptures available at that time. Rather than seeking a psychological methodology, they relied on revealed truth. They believed Jesus' words when He said, "If ye continue in my word, then are ye my disciples indeed; and ye shall know the truth, and the truth shall make you free" (John 8: 31,32). They counted on Christ working in and through them as He had clearly explained in His analogy of the vine and the branches (John 15). They relied on the work of the Holy Spirit. They understood the centrality of the spiritual life, of Christ in them. When they drifted into following the ways of men, the Apostle Paul wrote to them and urged them not to follow the wisdom of men, but to rely on the power of God (1 Corinthians 2:2-5; Colossians 2:6-10).

The spiritual ministry of caring for one another in the Body of Christ later became known as the "cure of souls" or the "care of souls." Such care depended upon the Word of God to understand the condition of man and minister relief for troubled minds. The "cure of souls" ministered to all mental, emotional, and spiritual disturbances. It involved prayer and often consisted of giving godly wisdom, instruction, and encouragement (including practical helps which often speak louder than words) to assist believers with their beliefs, emotions, thoughts, values, attitudes, relationships, and behavior. In his book *A History of the Cure of Souls,* John T. McNeill describes it as "the sustaining and curative treatment of persons in those matters that reach beyond the requirements of the animal life."[3] Prior to the twentieth century, churches provided such personal ministry to those in need, and some still do.

We have chosen throughout this book to refer to this ministry as the *care of souls* for two reasons. First, *care of souls* is a clearer translation of *cura animarum*, which was the original designation in the early church. McNeill says:

> The primary sense of *cura* is "care," and it is readily applied either to the tasks involved in the care of a person or thing, or to the mental experience of carefulness or solicitude concerning its object.[4]

Second, although the phrase "cure of souls" has been the preferred translation in the past, because of its emphasis on curing sinful souls, Scripture deals with the full range of Christian experience. We prefer the designation *care of souls*, which is all-encompassing from salvation through sanctification and from ministry to the suffering soul to ministry to one another in the normal Christian life. Caring for souls involves both the "cure" from sin and death and the ongoing mutual care in the Body of Christ throughout the process of sanctification.

The care of souls is one of the oldest ministries of the church. Christ paid the price for sin through His own substitutionary death. Then He rose again to give new life to every believer. His death canceled the debt of sin. That is the initial cure for sin and hell-bound death. Christ's life in every believer provides the ongoing care, not only for each individual believer but for the entire

Body of Christ. Jesus Christ ministers directly to each believer and also indirectly through believers to one another. This is the outworking of the care of souls who "are builded together for an habitation of God through the Spirit" (Ephesians 2:22).

The first description of the church with members ministering to one another is found in Acts:

> Then they that gladly received his word were baptized: and the same day there were added unto them about three thousand souls. And they continued stedfastly in the apostles' doctrine and fellowship, and in breaking of bread, and in prayers. And fear came upon every soul: and many wonders and signs were done by the apostles. And all that believed were together, and had all things common; and sold their possessions and goods, and parted them to all men, as every man had need. And they, continuing daily with one accord in the temple, and breaking bread from house to house, did eat their meat with gladness and singleness of heart, praising God, and having favour with all the people. And the Lord added to the church daily such as should be saved (Acts 2:41-47).

They learned and "continued stedfastly in the apostles' doctrine." They lived according to the truth they were learning. Their fellowship was based on sound doctrine and their new relationship in Christ, and its hallmark was love. Their love was not limited to words and feelings but was lived out in practical ways through such sharing of possessions and goods that no one was lacking. They continued "daily with one accord in the temple," broke bread together, praised God together and prayed together. The mutual care was active from the inception of the church. Jesus' words to His disciples to love one another as He loved them established the essence of the care of souls. Jesus loved to the point of giving His life, and He calls believers to give themselves to each other. The care of souls is not limited to words, as important as they are in teaching doctrine; the care of souls includes practical acts of love, which are expressions of true faith and doctrine (Galatians 5:6).

James, the leader of the first Christian church in Jerusalem, wrote, "Confess your faults one to another, and pray one for another, that ye may be healed" (James 5:16). Biblical doctrines of confession, repentance, forgiveness, exhortation, encouragement, and comfort were taught and practiced in the early church. Doctrines of the believer's position in Christ and Christ in the believer and of the active work of the Holy Spirit were taught and followed. These spiritual ways of living the normal Christian life were also the believer's means to mental, emotional, and spiritual healing through the centuries. The cure and care of souls was the application of Scripture to the life of the believer through the ministries given to the church through the Holy Spirit.

God nurtures people who have been harmed and forgives those who have sinned and repented. The care of souls begins with a person's relationship with God through salvation by grace through faith, continues the process of sanctification, and results in changed attitudes, thoughts, emotions, motives, and behavior. However, the world systems of "science falsely so-called" (1 Timothy 6:20) have undermined the care of souls ministry and intimidated Christians by deceiving them into believing they are not qualified or able to help one another in the serious issues of life. Even pastors, who have been ordained to care for the sheep, have been deceived into thinking that one must attain the requirements, degrees, and licenses to practice psychology before they are qualified to counsel, even though the care of souls is the exclusive ministry of the church, according to the calling of God and the gift of grace.

Our concern continues to be this: that the cure of minds (the psychological way) has displaced the care of souls (the spiritual way). However, additional concerns have arisen. Various attempts to move the church back to a biblical means of caring for souls created a biblical counseling movement that in numerous ways reflects the psychological way. Many who call themselves "biblical counselors" are outright integrationists, who attempt to use both the Bible and psychological counseling theories and techniques. Still others who call themselves "biblical counselors" may be using more Bible than psychology, but they have allowed certain psychological theories and techniques to color their view of Scripture. Others who call themselves "biblical counselors" may eschew psychology, but nevertheless copy some of the practices of psychological counseling, such as charging a fee and establishing community counseling centers separated from churches (or in the church, but separated from other ministries in the church). Some "biblical counselors" even believe in and use psychological tests and thereby label Christians according to the bankrupt and useless wisdom of men.[5] Others who call themselves "biblical counselors" rely on, promote, and even require specialized training for even the most mature believers before they can minister godly counsel.

In this volume we hope to encourage Christians to minister to one another in the Body of Christ on the basis of what the Bible teaches about personal ministry and the efficacy of mutual care. Today the two greatest obstacles to personal ministry are psychological counseling (and all it pretends to be) and the intimidation that comes from the biblical counseling movement, which has set up its own training programs and certificates. The primary reason churches do not minister personally to the soul struggling with problems of living is because of fear—fear that individuals who are not formally trained cannot handle people's problems and fear that criticism might be directed at the church for even trying. This is an example of Proverbs 29:25, "The fear of man bringeth a snare: but whoso putteth his trust in the LORD shall be safe." Since that fear is so universal, we have been compelled to speak out against psychological counseling, along with its underlying theories about who man is and how he changes. More recently we have expressed our concern about the biblical counseling movement, which has set up its own formal training and certificates.

We contend that the ordinary believer, who is indwelt by the Holy Spirit and has found the Lord and His Word sufficient in his life, is equipped to minister to a fellow believer who is struggling with personal issues of the soul. The high calling of the care of souls is also a common calling for all believers. As we emphatically state in *Against Biblical Counseling: For the Bible*:

> **Any person who can be used by the Holy Spirit to lead another to salvation or along the way of sanctification is competent to be used by God to give wise counsel without needing specialized biblical counseling training.**[6]

The care of souls is inherent in Christ's command to love one another (John 15:12).

Fundamental Issues in Caring for Souls

This book is for Christians who want to know what the Bible says about ministering the care of souls to one another. God desires to transform believers into the image of Christ. Lack of biblical change is an indication of spiritual stagnation, and being transformed into the image of Christ is a sign of spiritual vitality. Life's experiences can motivate people to change in different directions. The care of souls ministry relies on the Word of God and the work of the Holy Spirit. Such inner, spiritual change involves the work of God and the response of the individual.

The care of souls ministry cannot rely on human effort or ingenuity, because it is really the work of God. God's love enables a believer to live in relationship to Him, to overcome sin and its consequences, and to be transformed into the image of Christ. God's love engenders trust, which leads to obedience to His Word. His love includes both mercy and truth, both grace and justice. For the care of souls to be truly biblical, love must be its hallmark, its means, and its direction because "God is love."

The care of souls cannot be reduced to formulas. Those who minister by formulas will fail, or they will succeed for reasons other than the formulas used. Any formulized care of souls will fall short of what true mutual care in the Body of Christ is—a creative, spiritual process involving a person who needs help and another person who will come alongside as God's instrument of mercy and truth.

What we present in this book is just one small glimpse of what is totally available in Scripture. We cannot say how to minister in each specific situation. The Bible covers every generality and each person is unique. Therefore, the primary work is that of the Holy Spirit within the individual, according to God's Word, which is living, effectual and applicable to every individual, every situation, and every struggle. The Scriptures and the Holy Spirit provide an infinite number of possible applications of truth to be ministered in love to each person in each situation. In the care of souls God's Word is ministered by the Holy Spirit through one who has been transformed by the Cross of Christ to one who by God's grace receives and obeys.

As we discuss the care of souls, you may discover that you are already ministering spiritual care to fellow believers, or you may find that the person who listens to you and prays for you is practicing the care of souls, without having identified it as such. On the other hand, you may notice how easily people direct those struggling with life's problems to professional counseling or to biblical counseling "experts," when what they need is the care of souls operating within their own church.

We pray that as you read this book, you will be encouraged to seek the springs of Living Water for yourself and for others. The Word of God and the work of the Holy Spirit provide power for caring for souls as people seek to overcome problems of living. The care of souls needs to be restored in churches immediately before more Christians are sent out to an alien world for psychological help or to fee-for-service "biblical counselors." If they are not already doing so, pastors and others who have this call of God on their hearts can and should begin personally caring for souls—not next month or next year, but immediately. The ministry of mutual care, given to edify the church and to glorify God, is a calling of God on the life of every believer.

> As every man hath received the gift, even so minister the same one to another, as good stewards of the manifold grace of God. If any man speak, let him speak as the oracles of God; if any man minister, let him do it as of the ability which God giveth: that God in all things may be glorified through Jesus Christ, to whom be praise and dominion for ever and ever. Amen (1 Peter 4:10-11).

Unless we as believers minister to one another according to the Word of God and the work of the Holy Spirit, we are doing a great injustice to fellow believers at least and a great damage at worst. Struggles of the soul and problems of living must be dealt with as spiritual problems with spiritual solutions.

2

Getting Past the Obstacles to Caring for Souls

Psychological counseling with its underlying psychologies is still one of the most subtle and dangerous deceptions in the church today. It is also one of the greatest obstacles to biblically caring for souls in the Body of Christ. Psychological counseling theories often determine how believers view Scripture and how they understand biblical doctrine. These deceptive ideas have been embraced under a clever disguise of science and medicine. As conservative churches, Bible colleges, and seminaries brought in psychological counseling theories and therapies, they simply added them to whatever belief system they had. Rather than trusting in the efficacy of preaching the pure Word of God, pastors have been borrowing from the world, preach psychologized sermons, offer psychologized Sunday School classes, promote 12-step groups, and refer their sheep to psychological hirelings.

Psychological counseling and its underlying psychologies are insidious intrusions into the Christian faith. Psychological counseling consists of secular theories and techniques which are "after the tradition of men" (Colossians 2:8). **They are man-made ideas that offer a counterfeit salvation and a counterfeit means of sanctification.** Our concern is with the part of psychology that uses man-made explanations, speculations, prescriptions, methods, mediations and manipulations to deal with the nature of man, how he should live, and how he can change.

As we have said elsewhere, psychological counseling is a limited (one to one), timed (50 minutes), fixed (one day a week), paid ($50 to $150 per hour), routine (one right after another), relationship that leaves little room for depth or creativity. Unfortunately many biblical counselors function the same way. This is not the way the care of souls should work.

In our book *PsychoHeresy: The Psychological Seduction of Christianity*,[1] we introduced a new term by which to identify this serious problem. We coined the term *psychoheresy*, because integrating psychological explanations about the nature of man and how he changes with the Bible is psychological heresy. We identified it as *heresy* because contaminating the Bible with the integration of man-made psychological theories and techniques departs from the fundamental truth of the Gospel. Psychological heresy involves teaching, trusting, and promoting unscientific and unproved psychological opinions in areas where the Bible has already spoken.

The psychological way has affected how people view the Bible as well as how they view themselves. While we continue to be concerned about Christians outrightly practicing psychotherapy, our growing concern is psychologically tainted biblical counseling. Testimonials of success and happiness appear to support every one of the over 450 different psychological systems of counseling. Testimonials of success and happiness also appear to support all kinds of biblical counseling look-alikes. However, few therapists or biblical counselors broadcast their failures, unless they begin touting a better method of counseling than they previously employed. Research cited in our book *PsychoHeresy* clearly reveals that psychological explanations about life and psychological methods of dealing with problems of living are questionable at best, detrimental at worst, and spiritual counterfeits at least. There is no need or excuse for any biblical ministry to draw from those tainted cisterns of psychology.

Just because secular psychologies have failures, contradictions, and anti-Christian biases, does it follow that counseling in the church is also contaminated? Unfortunately what has been labeled "Christian psychology" involves the very same confusion of contradictory theories and techniques as its secular source, and much of what is called "biblical counseling" does too. Well-meaning individuals who profess Christianity have gleaned ideas and techniques from secular psychology. They may counsel what they believe to be the perfect blend of Christianity and psychology. Some admittedly use the theories and techniques devised by such men as Freud, Jung, Rogers, Janov, Ellis, Adler, Berne, Fromm, Maslow, and other theorists, none of whom embraced Christianity or developed a psychological system from the Word of God. Others simply worked those ideas into their own systems of what they call "biblical counseling." Some "Christian psychologists" have been more honest than others, as evidenced a number of years ago at the Christian Association for Psychological Studies (CAPS), when the following was admitted:

> We are often asked if we are "Christian psychologists" and find it difficult to answer since we don't know what the question implies. We are Chris-

tians who are psychologists but at the present time there is no acceptable Christian psychology that is markedly different from non-Christian psychology. It is difficult to imply that we function in a manner that is fundamentally distinct from our non-Christian colleagues . . . as yet there is not an acceptable theory, mode of research or treatment methodology that is distinctly Christian.[2]

Most claim to have taken only those elements of psychology that fit with Christianity. But, they are not consistent with one another in what they consider biblical. Even those who are highly critical about some aspects of psychology may, indeed, have absorbed aspects of the psychological way as each one developed his own individual method of counseling. **Recycling or modifying bankrupt systems of ungodly and unscientific theories and therapies will not make them biblical.**

Christ did not simply give believers a set of principles to follow; nor did He provide a means for people to analyze any particular person's soul. Instead, He gave Himself. He said, "I am the bread of life: he that cometh to me shall never hunger; and he that believeth on me shall never thirst" (John 6:35). Jesus is "the way, the truth, and the life," not Freud, Jung, Adler, Rogers, Maslow, or Ellis or any other such men. Jesus, the Apostles, and the early church did not send sheep out to feed in other pastures. Jesus offered Himself as the bread of life, and He continues to give the pure water of the Word springing up into eternal life.

Pastors, teachers, and counselors who have been influenced by the psychological way may not even realize the extent of that insidious influence or be concerned about its dangers. While some have purposefully added the psychological wisdom of men, others have done so through mindlessly absorbing psychological influences in the culture and in the church. Although not all pastors, Christian leaders, Bible college and seminary professors, and other Christians have been seduced by psychology, the psychological seduction of Christianity has a deep and broad impact, including the pastor's office, a vast counseling referral system, college and seminary classes, media and literature geared to a Christian audience, sermons, and even ordinary conversations among Christians.

Psychotherapies and their underlying psychologies constitute religion rather than science. In attempting to change the inner man, they intrude into God's territory. They contradict and interfere with God's means of transforming the inner man. By offering various other means of change, they subvert the Gospel and bypass the Cross and the resurrected life. Because they are man-made, humanistic religions, psychotherapies are religions of works. Paul urged believers to walk in Christ and have nothing to do with worldly means of growth and change:

> As ye have therefore received Christ Jesus the Lord, so walk ye in him: Rooted and built up in him, and stablished in the faith, as ye have been taught, abounding therein with thanksgiving. Beware lest any man spoil you through philosophy and vain deceit, after the tradition of men, after the rudiments of the world, and not after Christ (Colossians 2:6-8).

Believers are to walk in Christ, "rooted and built up in him, and stablished in the faith, as ye have been taught, abounding therein with thanksgiving." What a contrast to the complexities of the religions of psychotherapy and their underlying psychologies!

We want to free Christians from their attachment to psychology and their confidence in the process of counseling so that they might seek the Lord and follow His Word in their circumstances, personal struggles, and concerns. The Lord Himself is the Christian's source for living and confronting problems. The Bible gives the only accurate understanding of why man is the way he is and how he is to change. The Lord and His Word provide all that is necessary for life and godliness.

> Grace and peace be multiplied unto you through the knowledge of God, and of Jesus our Lord, According as his divine power hath given unto us all things that pertain unto life and godliness, through the knowledge of him that hath called us to glory and virtue: Whereby are given unto us exceeding great and precious promises: that by these ye might be partakers of the divine nature, having escaped the corruption that is in the world through lust (2 Peter 1:2-4).

Getting Past the Intimidation

Rather than simply returning to the care of souls ministry, Christians who wanted to use the Bible rather than secular counseling theories and therapies developed "biblical counseling." Unfortunately the biblical counseling movement has turned personal ministry and the care of souls into a limited conversation of counseling. Furthermore, in attempting to create an alternative to psychological counseling, they created a counseling look-alike with people designated as "counselors" and "counselees" and they developed various methods of "counseling." Next came the "counseling" ministries, which soon became specialized ministries separated from other ministries of the church. If a youth pastor, for instance, encounters a problem that appears to need "counseling," he would be made to feel inadequate if he has not been trained in pastoral or biblical counseling. Then, instead of ministering, he would refer the youth and perhaps the youth's family to a pastor specializing in biblical counseling. We call that intimidation!

Yes, believers, including pastors, are intimidated by so-called biblical counseling models and methods as well as by psychological models and methods. Without some specialized training in biblical counseling, they feel inadequate and refrain from ministering to fellow believers. Conversely, believers resist personal ministry from fellow believers, because they are "not qualified" on the basis of training and counseling experience. They seek the "experts" because they trust "experts" with their models and methods more than the work of the Holy Spirit through an ordinary believer.

The way many Christians have dealt with the intimidation and feelings of inadequacy has been to seek training in psychology, biblical counseling, or a combination of the two. Some report that they are much more secure counseling fellow believers after having taken a class and having a manual at their fingertips. Pastors and others who desire to minister biblically are thus seeking training in biblical counseling, when what they really need is knowing, understanding, and obeying the Word; having confidence to discard all psychotherapy; and relying on the sufficiency of Christ and the whole counsel of God. Christians would do well to follow Paul's admonition:

> And this I pray, that your love may abound yet more and more in knowledge and in all judgment; That ye may approve things that are excellent; that ye may be sincere and without offence till the day of Christ; Being filled with the fruits of righteousness, which are by Jesus Christ, unto the glory and praise of God (Philippians 1:9-11).

Believers who are studying the Word as "a workman that needeth not to be ashamed, rightly dividing the word of truth" (2 Timothy 2:15), walking according to the Spirit, and growing in the knowledge of Jesus Christ may have confidence in the One who lives in and through them to guide them as they have opportunities to minister to one another.

We urge every Christian who says, "I need special training to counsel biblically," to look at what the Word of God says about ministering to one another. Have you ever preached, taught a Sunday School class, or presented the Gospel message to an individual? Has the

Lord ever used you to convert a sinner or reprove one who is saved? Have you ever come alongside to encourage a fellow believer in righteousness or repentance? Have you ever shared the comfort of the Lord whereby you yourself have been comforted? Have you ever led another Christian to the same well of living water from which you drink? Have you loved and encouraged fellow believers through practical helps, such as giving food, helping them move, or giving hospitality? Are you willing to think and speak biblically and talk about practical theological matters when needful situations arise? Are you increasingly living by faith in Christ as evidenced by your attitudes and actions? As believers grow in Christ they should be able to answer "yes" to more and more of these kinds of questions. The flow of life from the Lord to one another in the Body of Christ should be happening on a regular basis.

Ministering versus Counseling

Is there really a difference between ministering and counseling? Is the difference greater than one of semantics or personal preferences? The practice of counseling is so ingrained in this world, that it is difficult for most people to imagine dealing with problems of living without a process called "counseling" and without persons designated as "counselors" and "counselees." While the word *counsellor* is used in Scripture, the meanings differ from the usual twentieth-century use of the word. Moreover, neither the Old nor New Testament has an equivalent for the word *counselee*. The term was not even in existence until 1934, when professional counselors needed a word to identify the recipients of their counseling. Much of what is called "biblical counseling" comes from the world rather than the Word.

We hope to make the differences clear throughout this book. However, a brief glimpse can be seen by considering the way some counseling centers attempt to be biblical, yet follow the ways of the world. An article written by a counselor at a well-known center of biblical counseling, who is also a trainer of biblical counselors and the editor of a well-known journal of biblical counseling, responds to a question asked by a counseling student. The student asked, "What do you do to prepare for a counseling session? And why do you prepare in the ways that you do?"

The author's answer involves such godly activities as prayer and confession, but it also reveals the vast difference between counseling and ministering. First of all this counseling center charges fees for counseling. No payment means no counseling. This fee-for-service has been a concern of ours for quite some time. Nevertheless this author together with those at the biblical counseling center continue to charge counseling fees. If a "counselee" cannot afford to pay, he is encouraged to get his her church to pay for the service. After all this is what the professional counselors in the world do.

Second, this center is separated from the church and operating in lieu of the church. This is unbiblical since the care of souls ministry is a function of the local church, not a business separated from the church. This counseling center obviously serves churches that are not functioning as the Body of Christ. If they were, they would have no reason to send members out to a pay-for-service counseling center, be it straight psychological counseling or recycled psychological counseling called "biblical counseling." While this center may be providing services where ministry is lacking, they are not ministering according to biblical guidelines for ministry as outlined in Ephesians 4, but are counseling instead. The place for the care of souls is clearly the church under leadership and mutually ministered by one another:

> And he gave some, apostles; and some, prophets; and some, evangelists; and some, pastors and teachers; for the perfecting of the saints, for the work of the ministry, for the edifying of the body of Christ: till we all come in the unity of the faith,

and of the knowledge of the Son of God, unto a perfect man, unto the measure of the stature of the fulness of Christ (Ephesians 4:11-13).

The Bible does not list "counselors" as ministry gifts to the church, "counselees" as recipients being perfected, or "counseling" as a function separated from other ministries in the Body of Christ. Here the Scripture refers to the work of apostles, prophets, evangelists, pastors, and teachers. Elsewhere Scripture refers to bishops, elders, deacons, and also to the priesthood of all believers participating in mutual care. Nevertheless, throughout the article mentioned above and in this counseling center and its publications, there are constant references to counselors, counselees, and counseling. They do not refer to fellow believers ministering to other believers in need of help. Moreover, as with all biblical counseling centers, the preparation of the "counselors" is directed towards the conversation between, to use their words, the *counselor* and the *counselee*. The stress and the direction is towards using the mouth and **not** the hands or feet.

Individuals who seek counsel often have a variety of needs, including food, money, clothing, child care, transportation, household furniture, appliances, and simply friendship. What has happened in the biblical counseling movement, which views believers as *counselees* being *counseled* by *counselors*, is that it becomes a paid conversational relationship rather than a godly functional relationship. Conversation becomes the sole means of ministry. In a biblical counseling center a believer who needs more than lip service will not be served, because biblical counseling, particularly in biblical counseling centers, has become a reflection of psychological counseling with its fee-for-service, one-right-after-another, one-up-one down pattern. While biblical counselors like to think they are biblical, they often are a mere reflection of psychological counseling in one or more ways. While they may say, "Be warm," we wonder how many provide the coats and blankets.

Yes, conversation is important, especially in ministering the Word of God to a fellow believer. However, that conversation should be in the context of the full range of mutual care in the Body of Christ. That conversation should be under the leadership and direction of the local fellowship. That conversation should be among believers who love one another and serve one another on an on-going basis where all have opportunities to serve and all have opportunities to receive. Finally, believers are to always be ready to give a reason for the hope that is in them. They are always to be available to give a word or perform service in season and out of season. All need to be ready to minister, not only when one anticipates a need or a planned conversation, but whenever the need or occasion to converse arises.

Training and Experience?

The response of many Christians may be "yes, but ." Those who yet fear assisting fellow believers overcome problems of living may be encouraged by the research that compares trained and untrained psychological counselors and that compares experienced and inexperienced counselors. Truax and Mitchell state: "There is no evidence that the usual traditional graduate training program has any positive value in producing therapists who are more helpful than nonprofessionals."[3] After reviewing psychotherapy outcome research, Morris Parloff concludes that there is no "convincing evidence that these procedures can be uniquely applied only by members of professions who have completed specified training programs and have honed their skills by lengthy experience."[4] Researcher Jerome Frank reveals the shocking fact of "the inability of scientific research to demonstrate conclusively that professional psychotherapists produce results sufficiently better than those of nonprofessionals."[5]

Hans Strupp at Vanderbilt University compared the results of trained and untrained therapists counseling two groups of male college students, who were equated on the basis of mental-emotional distress. Five psychiatrists and psychologists comprised the first group of therapists. "The five professional therapists participating in the study were selected on the basis of their reputation in the professional and academic community for clinical expertise. Their average length of experience was 23 years." The second group of "therapists" was made up of seven college professors from a variety of fields, but without therapeutic training. Each untrained "therapist" used his own personal manner of care, and each trained therapist used his own brand of therapy. The students seen by the professors showed as much improvement as those seen by the highly experienced and specially trained therapists.[6] There are many other examples like this in the literature.[7]

In his book *The Shrinking of America: Myths of Psychological Change,* psychotherapist Dr. Bernie Zilbergeld argues "that most problems faced by people would be better solved by talking to friends, spouses, relatives or anyone else who appears to be doing well what you believe you're doing poorly." After reviewing a great amount of research, Zilbergeld says:

> If I personally had a relationship problem and I couldn't work it out with my partner, I wouldn't go and see a shrink. I would look around me for the kind of relationship I admire. I wouldn't care if he was a carpenter or a teacher or a journalist . . . or a shrink. That's who I would go to. I want somebody who's showing by [his] life that [he] can do it.[8]

While some of the previous studies were conducted some years ago, no one has come up with substantial research to refute them. Robyn Dawes provides updates on research regarding training and experience in his book *House of Cards: Psychology and Psychotherapy*

Built on Myth. In discussing the huge and impressive Smith and Glass meta-analysis regarding the efficacy of psychotherapy, Dawes reports that "they discovered that the therapists' credentials—Ph.D., M.D., or no advanced degree—and experience were *un*related to the effectiveness of therapy."[9] He further explains:

> In the years after the Smith and Glass article was published, many attempts were made to disprove their finding that the training, credentials, and experience of therapists are irrelevant. These attempts failed. . . . In other words, the profession-als are not different from the paraprofessionals [amateurs] in the effectiveness of their treat-ment.[10]

One review of the research even went so far as to say that the professionally trained therapist is **as** effective as those who are only minimally trained, since some of the previous research results actually made the untrained, inexperienced person appear superior.[11]

If unbelievers who are neither psychological trained nor experienced have, on the average, as much success as psychologically trained and experienced therapists in giving personal care outside the Body of Christ, why should believers who are indwelt by Christ and have the Word of God fear ministering to one another? Christians must recognize that they are already in a unique training program that the world can only counterfeit. Christians are trained directly by the Lord through His Word and the Holy Spirit from the moment of their new birth, and they grow in experience with Him as they walk in fellowship with Him.

As believers live in relationship to God in such a way as to reflect His character and to prove His perfect will in day-to-day challenges of living they are being trained to minister. As believers study, understand, and apply the Word of God through obedience, they learn to live according to God's plan. Then, as they learn to live according to their new life in Christ, as revealed in

Scripture and by the power of the Holy Spirit, they are enabled to guide others along the same path. As believers progressively know the way through the love of God, knowledge of the Bible, and the experience of walking after the Spirit, they are able to lead others along the same path. They are competent to minister by God's grace through faith.

Encouraging the Care of Souls Ministry

The Lord Himself works in and through believers for His glory. As believers learn the Word of God, meditate on it, obey it, and practice it in the circumstances of life, they become prepared to minister life to another person. As they live according to the Word of God and walk according to the Spirit, they will find opportunities to minister according to the grace of God. From the day of Pentecost to today, the Lord has equipped His servants to minister and care for one another in the Body of Christ, but the biblical care of souls has suffered whenever man-made means of sanctification have taken precedence over God's ways.

The care of souls continues as believers do care for one another; as they pray, listen, encourage and, exhort one another; and as they have opportunities to teach and preach the Word of God. Yet, until the intimidation is shaken, believers will still be hesitant to care for one another through difficult trials and deep struggles of the soul. Believers need to renew their confidence in Christ as He lives in them and ministers through them.

What we emphatically stated before can be expanded to say: **Any person who is saved and growing through sanctification can be used by the Holy Spirit to lead another to salvation or along the way of sanctification and can be used by God to minister to fellow believers without specialized training.** Mutual care in the Body of Christ is more than giving wise counsel; it is ministering God's grace and truth whenever and wherever there is a need. Such ministry flows from one who is abiding in Christ just as a branch bears fruit as it abides in the vine, because all true ministry originates from God and all ministry is for His purpose and His glory.

The biblical care of souls involves more than just biblical conversation, it involves biblically caring for the whole person. Such care can be as simple as a cup of water given to a thirsty traveler or as complex as helping a family get through a crisis. It can be as gentle as a touch on the shoulder or as strong as a rebuke rightly rendered in love and truth. It can be working through issues with the Bible in one hand and a shovel in the other. Caring for souls entails so much variety in a multitude of circumstances that enumerating all the possibilities would be impossible. The Lord Jesus, who knows the heart of every believer and every detail about each one's life and circumstances, is "the head over all things to the church, which is his body, the fulness of him that filleth all in all" (Ephesians 1:22,23). Therefore believers can trust Him to orchestrate the care and to enable each believer to contribute to what might be lacking in another believer as the church edifies itself in love for the glory of God. Because of Christ, believers are competent to care for one another in Him.

This book is written to encourage Christians to do what believers did before being intimidated away from the care of souls. The message today seems to be loud and clear from many individuals and organizations not to minister in this area of the care of souls. Our purpose is to encourage such ministry in contrast to so many who discourage it by requiring believers to learn a number of verses or receive a certificate, diploma or degree. We say, **Minister! Do it if you have been born of the Spirit and are growing according to God's Word**.

3

Every Believer Called and Competent to Minister

When we consider fellow believers who influenced our Christian growth, many of us will find that those believers were not the ones who simply talked about their faith. They lived the Christian life. They loved and served in humility and faith. They may never have said anything tremendously profound or exegeted a passage of Scripture in our hearing, but they lived those Scriptures and thus communicated the essence of the Word. Yet, many believers consider themselves unequipped to minister. Unless they have taken various courses and earned certificates or degrees they stand on the sidelines and hope that someone else, such as the pastor or other church leader, will witness to an unbeliever, because they know the "right words" to say, or will help a fellow believer who is experiencing problems of living.

Numerous ministries have attempted to equip believers by supplying workshops, workbooks, and other helps. But, instead of such helps releasing Christians to minister, they have become impediments. The message that comes across is that Christians must have more training, more experience, more knowledge **before** they can minister. However, every believer already has the primary requirement for ministry— Jesus! He has given them new life and has come to live in them. Therefore, they can begin to serve as soon as they are born again.

Rather than following the notion that you must "know it all" before you minister, we encourage believers to step out in faith and minister before they "know it all." Whether you are a babe in Christ or a mature believer, you are competent to minister according to the grace of God whenever opportunities arise. While not all believers will be called and equipped to minister in leadership positions as pastors, elders, or teachers, ministry is for every member. Those in leadership positions must be mature in the faith and know Scripture well, but one does not have to be a pastor or elder to participate in witnessing the grace and truth of God to unbelievers or in mutually caring for one another in the Body of Christ. Every member of Christ's Body belongs to the priesthood of all believers and will bear fruit in ministry because of being in Christ.

The second requirement for ministry is also found in Jesus. It is humility. Jesus says:

> Come unto me, all ye that labour and are heavy laden, and I will give you rest. Take my yoke upon you, and learn of me; for I am meek and lowly in heart: and ye shall find rest unto your souls. For my yoke is easy, and my burden is light (Matthew 11:28-30).

What a picture of ministry—being yoked together with Jesus in whatever service to which He calls His disciples!

Peter urges believers to "be clothed with humility: for God resisteth the proud, and giveth grace to the humble. Humble yourselves therefore under the mighty hand of God, that he may exalt you in due time" (1 Peter 5:5-6). If we suppose that we can accomplish great things for God by our own intellectual or spiritual prowess, we are sadly mistaken. Jesus said, "Without me ye can do nothing" (John 15:5). We are dependent on the Lord in all we do whenever we serve.

But even here we cannot wait until we have enough humility before we can minister. The task of ministry should humble every believer, because no one is adequate for the task without the Lord. Yet, in Christ all believers can minister. Paul expresses it this way: "I can do all things through Christ which strengtheneth me" (Philippians 4:13). While Paul was speaking about how Christ enabled him to be content in all circumstances, the truth of the verse extends to all the Christian life. As believers confront situations and opportunities to minister, they must realize first that they are not adequate in themselves. Yet, at the same time they can rest in the fact that Christ in them is more than adequate to minister. Such knowledge is both humbling and empowering. Self is humbled and faith is enlarged, so much so that Blaise Pascal once wrote:

> Do little things as if they were great, because of the majesty of the Lord Jesus Christ who dwells in thee; and do great things as if they were little and easy, because of His omnipotence.

The scope of the care of souls ministry is far greater than the conversation of counseling. It includes words of encouragement, acts of kindness, prayers, and a multitude of other activities of the normal Christian life. As each believer lives the Christian life in fellowship with other believers, ministry will flow. Much of it will not even appear to be "ministry," but it is, if it builds up the Body of Christ. Participation in the care of souls by every believer is the biblical norm and works according to the description in Ephesians 4:16:

> From whom [Christ] the whole body fitly joined together and compacted by that which every joint supplieth, according to the effectual working in the measure of every part, maketh increase of the body unto the edifying of itself in love.

Notice particularly the phrase "the effectual working in the measure of every part." Every member serving effectively! And, that includes every member from babes in Christ to those who are growing more and more into the likeness of Christ.

Christ Our Example for Ministry

On the eve before His crucifixion Christ taught His disciples by word and by example. Jesus both demonstrated and explained the importance of humility by taking on the role of a lowly servant.

> Now before the feast of the passover, when Jesus knew that his hour was come that he should depart out of this world unto the Father, having loved his own which were in the world, he loved them unto the end. And supper being ended, the devil having now put into the heart of Judas Iscariot, Simon's son, to betray him; Jesus knowing that the Father had given all things into his hands, and that he was come from God, and went to God; He riseth from supper, and laid aside his garments; and took a towel, and girded himself. After that he poureth water into a basin, and began to wash the disciples' feet, and to wipe them with the towel wherewith he was girded (John 13:1-5).

Luke recorded that there had been strife among the disciples regarding "which of them should be accounted the greatest" (Luke 22:24). Jesus responded to the strife by saying:

The kings of the Gentiles exercise lordship over them; and they that exercise authority upon them are called benefactors. But ye shall not be so: but he that is greatest among you, let him be as the younger; and he that is chief, as he that doth serve (Luke 22:25-26).

He taught them, by word and example, the place of service and the requirement of humility.

Washing feet was the task of the lowliest servant in Israel. For Jesus to take the towel and begin to wash His disciples feet would have been shocking to them. Thus Peter blurted out: "Lord, dost thou wash my feet?" (John 13:6).

Jesus answered somewhat enigmatically, "What I do thou knowest not now; but thou shalt know hereafter" (John 13:7). The disciples could not yet comprehend the import of this seemingly insignificant task and what it demonstrated about Christian leadership and service. Peter revealed his lack of understanding when he foolishly declared, "Thou shalt never wash my feet" (John 13:8).

But Jesus, both Lord and Master, even as He took the position of the lowliest servant, said to Peter, "If I wash thee not, thou hast no part with me" (John 13:8).

In spite of Peter's lack of understanding, he expressed his utmost desire to have a part with Jesus by declaring, "Lord, not my feet only, but also my hands and my head" (John 13:9).

The foot washing demonstrated that ministry requires a willingness to take the lowliest position for the sake of one another in the Body of Christ. Once a person is saved and given new life he is clean, but, because he is still in the world, he will pick up the dirt of the world. Humble service to one another will serve to cleanse that external filth.

Jesus saith to him, he that is washed needeth not save to wash his feet, but is clean every whit: and ye are clean, but not all. For he knew who should

betray him; therefore said he, Ye are not all clean.
So after he had washed their feet, and had taken
his garments, and was set down again, he said
unto them, Know ye what I have done to you? Ye
call me Master and Lord: and ye say well; for so I
am. If I then, your Lord and Master, have washed
your feet; ye also ought to wash one another's feet.
For I have given you an example, that ye should do
as I have done to you (John 13:10-15).

Notice here that Jesus girded a towel, took a the position of a servant, and served. This is a picture of the
care of souls in action.

While some groups of believers practice foot washing in their attempt to follow His example, Jesus' example went beyond literal foot washing. Any service, done
in humility and love to a fellow believer, that removes
any contamination of the world and draws him closer to
the Lord follows our Lord's example. No wonder the
disciples could not initially understand their Master's
seemingly outlandish act. They did not yet know what it
would be like to be indwelt by Christ, to live His life as
expressed by Paul in Galatians 2:20, or to be part of a
new living entity: the Body of Christ. They did not have
a vision of the church or how it would function, for
Christ had not yet died and risen again. The full import
of Christ's simple act would only be realized after the
birth of the church.

Christ is both our example and our life. He lives in
us, and we desire to be like Him and to think His
thoughts. Scripture says that we become like Him by
looking at Him (2 Corinthians 3:18). As we watch Him,
we begin to act as He would act. As believers grow more
like Jesus, they also become examples. They become
living epistles as they reflect the life of Jesus in them
through faith and obedience (2 Corinthians 3:2,3). They
also become examples to the extent that Paul urges
believers: "Those things, which ye have both learned,
and received, and heard, and **seen in me**, **do**: and the

God of peace shall be with you" (Philippians 4:9, emphasis added). Believers in the Body of Christ learn to live the Christian life through precept and example, through hearing and seeing, and then through trusting and obeying.

With this idea in mind, we suggest that much ministry of mutual care comes simply through living the Christian life according to the power of God and the standards of Scripture. The following is one such example of a Christian ministering to fellow believers through a simple act of love.

A Glass of Water

A young couple, whom we will call Bill and Wendy, had been married about a year. Both had grown up in broken families and were fairly new Christians. They began attending church, but their marriage relationship was in serious trouble. They sought help. The pastor suggested that they begin meeting with a mature couple in the church. The mature couple, whom we will call Jack and Priscilla, had known the Lord for a number of years and the fruit of the Spirit was evident in their lives. Jack is an enthusiastic Christian with both wisdom and discernment. Priscilla has the gift of hospitality and graciousness. They have both found the Lord and His Word sufficient in their own lives and do not look to psychological theories or techniques either for themselves or for ministry. Jack and Priscilla graciously invited Bill and Wendy to their home.

Besides teaching Scriptures regarding marriage and describing the Christian life, Jack and Priscilla were simply loving Bill and Wendy as fellow believers. Whenever Bill and Wendy went to Jack and Priscilla's home, they observed their ways of relating to each other and to them. They saw Christ's love in action. They saw God's Word lived out, not as a performance act, but simply as they lived the normal Christian life.

Wendy told us the story about one evening when Priscilla had invited them to dinner. During the meal,

without a request and without a word, Priscilla got up
from the table, went into the kitchen, and returned with
a pitcher of water. She poured water into Jack's glass.
Wendy, who is quite inquisitive and not fearful about
asking questions, asked Priscilla why she did that.

Priscilla asked, "Did what?"

Wendy clarified her question. "Why did you go to the
kitchen, get the pitcher, and pour water into Jack's
glass?"

Priscilla seemed rather surprised to be asked such a
question. She answered, "It's just something I do."

"But he didn't ask for water," Wendy responded.

Priscilla smiled and explained that she noticed how
the water in his glass was low and that she thought he
would probably like some more.

Wendy confessed that she didn't see the sense in
that. Why should any woman wait on her husband that
way? Soon it was apparent that neither Bill nor Wendy
understood mutual care and service to one another in
marriage. They did not realize how they could express
love through small acts of kindness.

Both Bill and Wendy attribute the turnaround of
their marriage to that simple act of pouring water.
From observing that ordinary act of service and learning the essence of serving one another in love, they
moved from competitive self-seeking to putting each
other first. At first they consciously held that glass of
water as an example in their minds, but soon they
developed an eagerness to serve one another. They have
continued growing in Christ, not only in their marriage,
but in service within the Body of Christ. Now the pastor
sends young couples to Bill and Wendy.

We never know what the Lord will use as we do His
will and speak according to His Word. Priscilla would
never have guessed that pouring that glass of water for
Jack would have been used so mightily by the Lord. The
Lord may never use that act in the same way again, but
Priscilla continues to fill Jack's water glass, because she
desires to serve him in the Lord.

When one considers the import of that one act of kindness in the lives of that young couple, one cannot help but think of opportunities for ministry within every Christian family. What children observe they will learn. They often learn what they see demonstrated every day more fully than anything taught by words alone. Every believer is involved in ministry more than they realize.

As soon as we are born again we belong to Christ. We are not our own any more. We are His (1 Corinthians 6:19), and we are to glorify God in our bodies. That is, we are to glorify God in whatever we do, because everything a Christian does concerns Christ and His Body. Jesus tells us, "Let your light so shine before men, that they may see your good works, and glorify your Father which is in heaven" (Matthew 5:16). This does not mean that we are to draw attention to ourselves or to what we are doing. Instead, we are simply to do that which is right in the Lord by grace through faith. Then when people see the good works that are born of faith in God, He will get the glory.

Rides to Church

The Lord provides numerous opportunities to minister to one another in the Body of Christ. So often we do not even realize that ministry is going on as we live our lives in one another's presence. We had the privilege of driving a retired missionary to church over a number of years. We were grateful for the opportunity to minister, but found that we, ourselves, and our children were the true recipients of ministry. What a strong testimony of faith was lived before us every time we saw her.

Through the conversations that naturally arose as we drove back and forth over a number of years, Mary shared her story in bits and pieces. We soon discovered that only a burning passion for Jesus could have sustained Mary through the years of hardship among the Lisu people in the mountain region of inland China. She and her husband, Alfred, had been called by God to minister to people who had never heard the Gospel of Jesus. After enduring the hardships of learning the language and becoming accustomed to vast differences in living conditions, they settled among the Lisu people in the mountainous region of inland China.

Their infant son died soon after he was born, and yet they stayed on. Mary's sister joined them and the work grew rapidly. After some fruitful years of ministry and many souls won to Christ, they sought additional workers. Mary took the long journey—three weeks by mule, then many days by train and weeks by boat—to England to inspire workers to come to China.

Soon after she returned to the mission, Alfred made plans to meet the young couple that had responded to Mary's invitation to work with them. Alfred and his closest Lisu worker, Pastor Ho, began the long journey to meet the new missionaries, but Alfred never completed the journey. Pastor Ho saw his beloved brother in the Lord swept away in the Mekong River.

He continued the journey alone and met the young couple. Then, after many weeks they reached the mission station to join the new widow, her children, and her sister. By this time Mary had two young daughters. It would have been logical for her to return to her own homeland. Logical, yes, but her love for Jesus and for the Lisu people, whom He had put in her care, kept her in China. She had come to serve her Lord.

Mary stayed in China with only a few furloughs, one of which was enforced by political problems. She continued while her daughters grew into womanhood. After graduating from Bible school, one of her daughters returned to China to minister with her mother. But only a few months after her arrival, she became ill and died. Yet Mary knew what it had cost the Father to give His only-begotten Son to save many souls, and so she stayed on as long as she could.

We saw in Mary a down-to-earth, practical devotion to her Lord. She was not at all "holier-than-thou," but she was stalwart in her commitment to her Lord. She knew how to laugh at herself and was not afraid to admit her mistakes and failings. Whenever she spoke, she expressed the faithfulness of God.

She told of one incident about when they were traveling in a caravan. They had been delayed in a small village an extra day, and she confessed, "I fussed in my spirit and I fussed in my spirit." Little did she realize at the time that the Lord had been sparing them, for, if they had traveled with the caravan the day they had planned, they would have been robbed by bandits. She would shake her head and say again, "And there I was fussing in my spirit while all along God was taking care of us."

Mary always wanted to be sure that she elevated the love and faithfulness of God rather than her own goodness. She did this because she knew Him intimately and had received much of His love and grace. She did this because her whole life was a love relationship with Jesus.

We believe the Lord used Mary's life in Him to give our children a desire to serve Him. One son is a now a pastor and one daughter is a missionary. Here was an example of mutual care in the Body of Christ. We ministered to her temporal needs—rides to church. She ministered to our spiritual needs—to know Christ more fully. This is what we have found over and over again. Whenever we have extended a hand to minister to a fellow believer, we have received from the Lord more than we gave.

Ministering by Letter

Ministry is in ordinary places, even though true ministry is supernatural in origin. What the Lord gives us is often the very thing that we can minister to others. A dear friend, who has come to know the Lord more fully and intimately as she has turned to Him in the midst of personal trials, suffered yet another loss. Her husband was suddenly killed in an automobile accident. She and her young daughters turned to the Lord

in their suffering and found Him sufficient. In her pain
of loss she drew yet closer to Christ and asked Him to
purify her through this trial, according to 1 Peter 1:7.

> That the trial of your faith, being much more
> precious than of gold that perisheth, though it be
> tried with fire, might be found unto praise and
> honour and glory at the appearing of Jesus Christ.

She sent me a copy of her letter to a family that had
just experienced a similar loss. With her permission we
reproduce it here:

> Dear _____ Family:
> The M_____ family told us of the recent loss of
> your dear wife/mother; you have been heavy on my
> heart and in my mind ever since.
> In this most difficult first year as a widow
> myself, I realize that the same affliction is being
> accomplished in fellow brethren as yourselves (1
> Peter 5:9). How my heart has ached not only for
> my family, but for your family also. When I pray
> for myself I immediately include your name, that
> God would be gracious unto us; that He would be
> our arm (of strength) every morning, our salvation
> also in the time of trouble (Isaiah 33:2). This is my
> comfort in my affliction; for Thy Word has revived
> me and given me life. Unless God's law had been
> my delight this last year, I should then have
> perished in mine affliction (Psalm 1:19:50,92).
> How firm a foundation is laid for our faith in His
> excellent Word! What more can He say than to us
> He has already said, to us who for refuge to Jesus
> have fled? Fear not, He is with us; O be not
> dismayed, for He is our God, and will still give us
> aid; He will strengthen us, help us, and cause us to
> stand, upheld by His righteous, omnipotent hand.
> 'When through fiery trials our pathway shall lie,
> God's grace all sufficient shall be our supply: The
> flame shall not hurt us, He only designs our dross

to consume and our **gold** to refine' (from "How Firm a Foundation").

Staying the mind on Jehovah, standing on the promises, and settling down on our Firm Foundation has been a relentless, weary battle of the mind for me. Girding up the loins of my mind, thinking soberly, and hoping to the end for the grace of God (1 Peter 1:13) has been challenging when the roaring lion walks about day and night seeking to defeat, disarm, and devour(1 Peter 5:9). But I can testify that resistance and perseverance are possible through Christ who strengthens me (Phil. 4:13); God's strength is made perfect in my weakness (2 Cor. 12:9); one can endure hardness as a good soldier of Jesus Christ (2 Tim. 2:1,3).

May both of our families be found faithfully submitting to the Refiner of our souls, that purged and perfected by these present fiery trials we all may come forth as **gold** unto praise, glory, and honor at the appearing of Jesus Christ (Job 23:10; 1 Peter 1:7).

Not everyone will minister in the same way as with such a letter, but correspondence is definitely a way to care for one another in the Body of Christ.

John 3:16

Many years ago we heard this next story told from the pulpit. We have lost the details of the story and its location, but will try to fill in without losing the essence of what happened. A successful businessman was in the midst of a business trip and attended a church in that locality. He did not usually go to church, but he had been troubled and hoped to find something there, although he did not know quite what.

The music was pleasing, but it did not quiet his heart or give him the solace he was seeking. He listened to the sermon, but his intellect argued the many points. Just as he was about to leave, a young man approached

him and confidently declared, "For God so loved the
world, that he gave his only begotten Son, that whosoever believeth in him should not perish, but have everlasting life."

The visiting businessman didn't see how God loved
the world in the first place and how giving His Son
could ever be connected with everlasting life, but the
young man persisted. He had no argument for the visitor. Instead he simply repeated the same words, "For
God so loved the world, that he gave his only begotten
Son, that whosoever believeth in him should not perish,
but have everlasting life."

Again the visitor explained further reasons why
that could not be so. His arguments revealed years of
university training, and his speech was articulate.
Nevertheless, his words seemed to have no effect on the
young man, who repeated again, "For God so loved the
world, that he gave his only begotten Son, that whosoever believeth in him should not perish, but have everlasting life."

The visitor continued to counter the young man's
words and each time heard the words of John 3:16
repeated in his ear. He realized that his opponent in
debate did not have the mind for intellectual discussion
or cogent arguments. At every turn the young man
repeated John 3:16. At last the visitor was struck by the
truth of those words. God burned those words into his
heart and gave him faith to believe. He got on his knees
and wept in gratitude for the truth of one Scripture, the
only Scripture the young man knew. God used the faithful ministry of a retarded young man and gave that visiting businessman new life.

She Gave What She Knew

The myth that believers must become experts before
they can minister is evident in this next story. A nurse,
who had walked with the Lord for a number of years,
was in conversation with another woman who was
working at the same hospital. The woman was experi-

encing problems of living and didn't know where to turn. When she shared her problems and frustrations, the nurse presented the Gospel and led her to Christ. The woman was converted and received faith to believe in Christ unto salvation. Yet the nurse did not feel adequate to help the woman with her problems. She asked us, and we encouraged her to proceed from where she began with the woman. Tell her what you know about living the Christian life, pray for her, bring her to church, study the Bible with her, help her grow in Christ. The nurse looked at us in surprise and relief. She knew that in Christ she could do those things, but she had been intimidated by the notion that people need professional counseling to overcome problems of living.

More than Fun and Games

Church programs often attempt to appeal to young people by offering entertainment, but young believers are often interested in more than fun and games. We have reports of high school and college groups pitching in to help wherever help is needed. One church newsletter says: "The College and Career Fellowship is offering its services to widows and others in need of help." The announcement is followed by a name and phone number. What kind of work do these young people do? These are some answers given by one of them:

> We have been involved in moving many different families in the church. We help them pack as well as load cars, trucks and vans. We also clean the old and new homes. We get a lot of calls to clean windows and gutters, and will clean just about anything else. We have raked a ton of leaves. You'd be amazed how fast a yard gets raked when 15 people go at it at once. We want to help those who have genuine needs. If you have prayed about a task and find it is more than you can handle, we are here to serve.

The Supernatural Ministry of Ordinary Believers

The care of souls is a supernatural ministry, but Christ uses ordinary Christians in whom He dwells to minister in a multitude of ways. Believers do not have to be afraid to minister to those in need. The Lord will supply. He will take what little a believer has to offer and enlarge it for His purpose. He who was able to take a young lad's bit of fish and bread and enlarge that small gift to feed a multitude is the same yesterday, today, and forever. He is able to take what we offer Him by faith in service to one another and use it for His glory. He is able to take the simple act of a wife pouring water into her husband's glass and change two hearts. He is able to take ordinary conversation and enrich lives. He is able to extend comfort through one to whom He has given comfort. He is not limited by a person's intelligence, but is able to give life through the best Gospel presentation a person can give. He is able to use believers of all ages who are "here to serve." Ministry is exercised in words and action, in season and out of season. It is the small or great multitudinous things believers can do that are used by the Holy Spirit to accomplish the supernatural work of God in the Body of Christ.

4

A High Calling;
A Common Calling

Caring for souls is a high calling. Nevertheless it is the calling of every Christian among the priesthood of all believers. No believer is exempt from mutually caring for one another in the Body of Christ. Although it is a high calling, it is possible for the humblest believer who is abiding in Christ. Caring for souls is a high calling, but it is also a common calling, one to which every believer is both called and equipped. However, although it is a common calling, it cannot be done by human wisdom, technical ingenuity, or scientific insight.

The care of souls through justification, regeneration, and sanctification is first of all God's domain. He uses preaching to save and sanctify. He is the One who justifies on the basis of Christ's sacrifice and sanctifies on the basis of Christ's Resurrection. He is the One who regenerates by giving new life to the believer. At the moment of new life, the believer becomes so related to Christ that he is a branch engrafted to a vine, and that vine is Christ.

Abiding in Christ

During His final hours with His disciples, Jesus explained what their life and ministry would be like by using an analogy of the vine. He said:

> Abide in me, and I in you. As the branch cannot bear fruit of itself, except it abide in the vine; no more can ye, except ye abide in me. I am the vine, ye are the branches: he that abideth in me, and I in him, the same bringeth forth much fruit: for without me ye can do nothing (John 15:4,5).

All true ministry begins with abiding in Christ, but what does that mean in relation to caring for souls? Abiding in Christ means to remain in Him and to continue in Him—to remain and continue to remain in the position of being **in** Christ, so that one lives and serves from that position of relationship rather than from a position of independence. A believer who is going to bear fruit ministers from his position in Christ. If he is to bear fruit, he does not attempt to care for another's soul apart from his position **in** Christ.

No one can bear spiritual fruit independently apart from Christ. One who ministers through abiding in Christ will not look to psychological theories or techniques that were developed by those who were not in Christ and who were not developing those ideas from a position of abiding in Christ. That is because ministry in the Body of Christ is spiritual. Its source is God the Father through His Word, His Son, and His Spirit. Paul exhorts the Galatian believers:

> Brethren, if a man be overtaken in a fault, ye which are spiritual, restore such an one in the spirit of meekness; considering thyself, lest thou

also be tempted. Bear ye one another's burdens, and so fulfil the law of Christ. For if a man think himself to be something, when he is nothing, he deceiveth himself (Galatians 6:1-3).

One who is spiritual is one in whom Christ lives and who is living in Christ. That is the singular qualification given here for the ministry of bearing one another's burdens—the single qualification for mutual care in the Body of Christ. Notice that this qualification has nothing whatsoever to do with training or degrees, how many verses one has memorized, or even how long one has been a believer. Within these few verses, the process of caring for one another is given simply: "restore such an one in the spirit of meekness." How does one restore another? In meekness, a fruit of the Spirit that comes from abiding in Christ. Meekness is the opposite of pride and self sufficiency.

The next step in the process, "considering thyself, lest thou also be tempted," is a reminder to depend upon Christ rather than self, recognizing that the flesh is weak, but that the Spirit gives life. Then comes the instruction for ministry: "Bear ye one another's burdens, and so fulfil the law of Christ."

Oh, what complications people have added to this simple ministry of caring for souls! But, when one attempts to minister from one's own expertise, one's own abilities, one's own training, one's own opinions, then there must be complexities and theories and techniques, because the one thing that is needful is missing! Yet, someone might ask, what if we add training and expertise and knowledge to abiding in Christ? If so, the training must be fully of Christ, the knowledge must be of Him, and humility must replace expertise, for Jesus clearly said, "Without me you can do nothing!" If there is any training or any knowledge it must be subservient to abiding in Christ and depending on Him to do the real inner work. No spiritual work is possible outside one's position in Christ, apart from abiding in Him and in His Word, or separated from Christ abiding in the one who is called to minister. Jesus had said earlier, "It is the spirit that quickeneth; the flesh profiteth nothing" (John 6:63).

Do you see what freedom this gives the believer who is to minister? Do you see what joy? Ministry becomes an opportunity to see fruit come forth from the vine, to see results coming forth from Christ, not from the wisdom or even the words of the believer who comes alongside to restore another in the spirit of meekness and to see Christ set that person free from sin and error.

Rather than taking classes in counseling or hunting for spiritual gems in the dung of psychogarble, a believer who desires to bear fruit and who is called to come alongside another must learn to abide in Christ. Abiding in Christ brings great confidence in Him rather than self-confidence. Those who have absorbed unbiblical psychological notions need to be pruned by the Lord. He even prunes healthy fruit-bearing Christians to make the fruit more excellent.

Abiding in Christ is that place of bearing fruit, becoming His disciple, obeying Him, experiencing spiritual intimacy, and living life to its fullest with joy (even while dying to self). Jesus said:

> If ye abide in me, and my words abide in you, ye shall ask what ye will, and it shall be done unto you. Herein is my Father glorified, that ye bear much fruit; so shall ye be my disciples. As the Father hath loved me, so have I loved you: continue ye in my love. If ye keep my commandments, ye shall abide in my love; even as I have kept my Father's commandments, and abide in his love. These things have I spoken unto you, that my joy might remain in you, and that your joy might be full (John 15:7-11).

Obedience to Christ is not to secure or maintain one's salvation, or to make it to heaven. Obedience to Christ is the result of His substitutionary death that brought salvation. Obedience is the response of love to the One who loved first. Obedience to Christ comes from knowing Him and abiding in Him. Then, as believers continue obeying Christ, they will experience what it is to abide, to live according to the position Christ gained for them, that is, to live **in** Christ. There believers will find abiding love and great joy in being spiritually and eternally connected to Christ.

Living in Christ is a spiritual condition, which acts upon the fact that a believer's position is in Christ. That marvelous position of being in Christ was provided by the Father through the death and Resurrection of His Son and is effected through faith which is given by God's grace. Paul speaks about that position in his letter to the Ephesians and "to the faithful in Christ Jesus" (Ephesians 1:1). He reminds those of us who are in Christ, that we have been blessed "with all spiritual blessings in heavenly places in Christ," that we were chosen "in him before the foundation of the world," that He "hath made us accepted in the beloved, in whom we have redemption through his blood, the forgiveness of sins, according to the riches of his grace; wherein he hath abounded toward us in all wisdom and prudence" (Ephesians 1:3,4,6-8). In Him we "obtained an inheritance" and have been "sealed with that holy Spirit of promise, which is the earnest of our inheritance until the redemption of the purchased possession, unto the praise of his glory" (Ephesians 1:11,13-14).

Paul also reminds us that we who were dead in sin have been made to "sit together in heavenly places in Christ Jesus." We who have been saved through faith "are his workmanship, created in Christ Jesus unto good works, which God hath before ordained that we should walk in them" (Ephesians 2:6,10). These good works include mutual care in the Body of Christ. Christians have no life apart from Christ and they can bear no fruit apart from Him, but through Him they can do all things (Philippians 4:13).

It is from this position of grace that we walk according to the Spirit, that we obey Christ Jesus, that we grow in our knowledge of Him, and that we become more like Him. As we abide in Christ we are to love the way He loves. He said: "This is my commandment, That ye love one another, as I have loved you" (John 15:12). Just hours before He went to the cross, He said: "Greater love hath no man than this, that a man lay down his life for his friends" (John 15:13). Christ put the well-being of others before His own comfort. He died in our place for our iniquity that we might live. He commands us to love one another to the same degree. Through this place of abiding in Christ and abiding in His love, He enables believers to minister to one another in love. That is what the care of souls is all about.

Edifying the Body in Love and Truth

After Jesus ascended to the Father He "gave gifts unto men" (Ephesians 4:8). The following verses list the gifts and their purpose:

> And he gave some, apostles; and some, prophets; and some, evangelists; and some, pastors and teachers; For the perfecting of the saints, for the work of the ministry, for the edifying of the body of Christ: Till we all come in the unity of the faith, and of the knowledge of the Son of God, unto a perfect man, unto the measure of the stature of the fulness of Christ: That we henceforth be no more children, tossed to and fro, and carried about with every wind of doctrine, by the sleight of men, and cunning craftiness, whereby they lie in wait to deceive; But speaking the truth in love, may grow up into him in all things, which is the head, even Christ: From whom the whole body fitly joined together and compacted by that which every joint

supplieth, according to the effectual working in the measure of every part, maketh increase of the body unto the edifying of itself in love (Ephesians 4:11-16).

These gifts are people whom God has called and equipped for serving the Body of Christ. Christ first gave the Apostles and prophets to build the foundation, of which He is the chief cornerstone. These are the Apostles and prophets of which Paul speaks earlier in Ephesians, when he tells Gentile believers:

> Now therefore ye are no more strangers and foreigners, but fellowcitizens with the saints, and of the household of God; And are built upon the foundation of the apostles and prophets, Jesus Christ himself being the chief corner stone; In whom all the building fitly framed together groweth unto an holy temple in the Lord: In whom ye also are builded together for an habitation of God through the Spirit (Ephesians 2:19-22).

Jesus gave the Apostles and prophets to establish the church. One requirement for an Apostle was to have seen the risen Lord Jesus. Today the words *apostle* and *prophet* are used in a more general sense, with an *apostle* being one sent to preach the Gospel and a *prophet* being one who speaks forth for God, within the constraints of the written Word.

The Lord gives evangelists, pastors and teachers to His church for three express purposes: "for the perfecting of the saints, for the work of the ministry, for the edifying of the body of Christ" (Ephesians 4:12). Christ gives evangelists to go forth and preach the Gospel to bring individuals to salvation. He gives pastors and teachers to bring those who are saved to maturity, along the process of sanctification. Christ gives gifts of ministry for specific purposes to fulfill specific goals. These gifts of ministry prepare the saints for service to build up the body of believers to maturity in the faith.

In Ephesians 4:11-12, Paul presents Christ's gifts to the church and says that these gifts equip the believers to serve and minister to one another in such a way that the Body of Christ is edified. Paul then details the goals that are to be accomplished in the church:

> Till we all come in the unity of the faith, and of the knowledge of the Son of God, unto a perfect man, unto the measure of the stature of the fulness of Christ: That we henceforth be no more children, tossed to and fro, and carried about with every wind of doctrine, by the sleight of men, and cunning craftiness, whereby they lie in wait to deceive; But speaking the truth in love, may grow up into him in all things, which is the head, even Christ (Ephesians 4:13-15).

Christ gives evangelists, pastors and teachers to train and equip the members of the Body of Christ so that they, in turn, can serve to build up the Body in the unity of the faith, in knowing Christ, in becoming established in the truth, and in becoming more and more like Him. The ministry of mutual care works like a living organism in which each part supplies what is necessary for the body. Nowhere in this list of ministering gifts is there a specified office of counselor. Nowhere in the process of equipping is there a psychotherapeutic mentality. Instead, there are evangelists who bring the Good News of salvation to those who are lost, and there are pastors and teachers who equip those who are saved so that they might build up one another in the faith until all come to maturity. Here is the picture of the ministry of mutual care.

When a member of the body suffers, the whole body suffers and will want to supply what is missing (1 Corinthians 12:26,27). There is no formula and there are no psychological techniques to be mastered. What is needed is mutual love and mutual caring so that each member grows in the common faith, in knowing Christ, in gaining stability through sound doctrine, and in becoming more like Christ. But without the supreme and sovereign work of the Lord in His Body and in each member of His Body, there would be no fruit or growth to maturity. While the Body actively works to build up itself in maturity through mutually caring for one another, it is Christ who does the major work through the Word of God and the Holy Spirit.

Christ gives the gifts of evangelists, pastors and teachers who train and equip the Body to edify itself. Christ is the head of the Body and directs the process of growth through the Holy Spirit and the Word of God. Moreover, Christ is the life of the Body. He provides all that is necessary for the saints to serve and thereby build up the body to spiritual maturity.

If a church becomes fragmented or if evangelists, pastors and teachers fail to dispense sound doctrine, members may be left stranded and deceived. Therefore those who hold positions of leadership have grave responsibilities to the Body of Christ. If they allow error to creep in and fail to speak the truth in love, they can do great harm to the believers. One of the results of fragmentation and error has been psychoheresy. In their zeal to fix broken lives, Christian leaders, who carry the responsibility of feeding the flock, have turned to psychology for help or they have emulated the therapeutic milieu. By doing so, they have undermined the faith, encouraged knowing self more than knowing Christ, succumbed to various winds of doctrine, and have stunted spiritual growth.

We are not calling the church back to an earlier era, but back to its foundation laid by the Apostles and prophets with Jesus Christ being the cornerstone—back to functioning according to the process described by Paul in Ephesians, Romans and 1 Corinthians—back to abiding in Christ as He described in His Words to His disciples as recorded in John 15.

While evangelists, pastors and teachers may give wise counsel from God's Word, there is no special designation of *counselor* as that term is commonly used in the twentieth century. Evangelists, pastors and teachers are all to be deeply involved in the care of souls by equipping the saints to serve for the edification of the Body. Since the purpose of ministry in the Body is to edify itself to spiritual maturity and since every part is to function towards that goal, all members have a part in caring for souls. The Reformers referred to the involvement of all believers in the care of souls as mutual care in the Body of Christ.

Ministering in the Body of Christ

Even new believers can minister. New believers and mature believers are all called to serve. Scripture is clear on this point:

> I beseech you therefore, brethren, by the mercies of God, that ye present your bodies a living sacrifice, holy, acceptable unto God, which is your reasonable service (Romans 12:1).

The first act of service is presenting oneself to God to use as He sees fit. This implies a full-time commitment, that God is Lord of every aspect of a person's life. Christianity is not a part-time volunteerism, but a readiness to obey and serve at all times within whatever occupation one has been given. Luther made this clear when he wrote, "Every shoemaker can be a priest of God and stick to his own last [block on which shoes are built or repaired] while he does it."[1] Paul urged all believers to be "always abounding in the work of the Lord, forasmuch as ye know that your labour is not in vain in the Lord" (1 Corinthians 15:58).

Paul describes how one is to serve God, not by the world's methods but by having one's mind transformed by God:

> And be not conformed to this world: but be ye transformed by the renewing of your mind, that ye may prove what is that good, and acceptable, and perfect, will of God (Romans 12:2).

Paul also teaches that all should be serving humbly, according to the grace and the measure of faith that have been given to them :

> For I say, through the grace given unto me, to every man that is among you, not to think of himself more highly than he ought to think; but to think soberly, according as God hath dealt to every man the measure of faith (Romans 12:3).

Although mature believers may have more faith, knowledge, experience, and opportunities, all believers should be encouraged to participate in mutually caring for one another, "according as God hath dealt to every man the measure of faith."

As every member of Christ's Body serves, all do so through God's enabling and equipping. God enables through the Holy Spirit; He equips with the Word of God and with spiritual gifts. Paul refers to his calling and equipping for ministry this way: "I was made a minister, according to the gift of the grace of God given unto me by the effectual working of his power" (Ephesians 3:7). Here Paul speaks of "the gift of grace." All gifting for ministry is by grace for service. No gift should be considered the property of the one who exercises the gift, but rather the property of Christ's Body. If an individual is used mightily by God in evangelizing, preaching, or teaching, he must realize that the gift of ministry, the enabling for ministry, and the fruit of that ministry are not one's own. They belong to God. That is why there is no place for arrogance in any true ministry.

Some of the ministry gifts are listed in Romans 12. Each can be expressed in many ways and circumstances for the mutual edification of believers.

For as we have many members in one body, and all members have not the same office: So we, being many, are one body in Christ, and every one members one of another. Having then gifts differing according to the grace that is given to us, whether prophecy, let us prophesy according to the proportion of faith; Or ministry, let us wait on our ministering: or he that teacheth, on teaching; Or he that exhorteth, on exhortation: he that giveth, let him do it with simplicity; he that ruleth, with diligence; he that showeth mercy, with cheerfulness (Romans 12:4-8).

This list includes prophecy, ministry, teaching, exhortation, giving, ruling, and showing mercy, but not counseling, especially not fee-for-service counseling.

The Gift of Prophecy
Prophecy here would be speaking forth for God. If one is to speak, preach or teach, he is to do so by what God has revealed in His Word. Peter says:

If any man speak, let him speak as the oracles of God; if any man minister, let him do it as of the ability which God giveth: that God in all things may be glorified through Jesus Christ, to whom be praise and dominion for ever and ever. Amen (1 Peter 4:11).

In the same sentence he connects speaking and ministry, because the source for both must be God Himself. For speaking must come from Scripture and ministry must come from "the ability which God giveth." That is because the glory is to go to God and not to the one who exercises God's gifts.

The Gift of Ministry
The *gift of ministry* is a general term, but, in the context of Romans 12 and also as presented in 1 Peter 4:11, it appears to refer to service that is done rather

than words that are spoken. Acts 6 records a problem that arose because of the rapid increase in the number of followers of Jesus, and thus began a broadening of leadership to oversee the ministry of serving tables.

> And in those days, when the number of the disciples was multiplied, there arose a murmuring of the Grecians against the Hebrews, because their widows were neglected in the daily ministration. Then the twelve called the multitude of the disciples unto them, and said, It is not reason that we should leave the word of God, and serve tables. Wherefore, brethren, look ye out among you seven men of honest report, full of the Holy Ghost and wisdom, whom we may appoint over this business. But we will give ourselves continually to prayer, and to the ministry of the word. And the saying pleased the whole multitude: and they chose Stephen, a man full of faith and of the Holy Ghost, and Philip, and Prochorus, and Nicanor, and Timon, and Parmenas, and Nicolas a proselyte of Antioch: Whom they set before the apostles: and when they had prayed, they laid their hands on them (Acts 6:1-6).

This ministry is physical service to edify the Body of Christ. The importance of what may appear to be mundane service can be seen by the fact that the Apostles chose "seven men of honest report, full of the Holy Ghost and wisdom" to oversee the fair distribution of material necessities. Through the division of labor among the believers, the Apostles were then free to give themselves "continually to prayer, and to the ministry of the word," which was their calling in service.

The gift of ministry involves every act of service in the mutual care of believers. It includes much of what believers do day by day in their own families. Parents minister to their children by giving them the physical necessities of life as well as love and godly instruction. They are performing ministry in the Body of Christ as they bring their children up "in the nurture and admonition of the Lord" (Ephesians 6:4).

The gift of ministry includes every act of kindness that comes from Christ and is exercised by a believer. It extends from painting the church building to working in the nursery, to caring for the children of an ill mother, to preparing meals for one another, to sewing clothes for the needy, to ushering, to giving rides, and on and on. There is no end to the possibilities, but it goes directly against anything that draws people to self-indulgence and to self-righteous involvement in "charities" to make people feel important or good about themselves. The gift of ministry is a spiritual gift for spiritual service to the glory of God. It is often unseen and unrecognized, but it should be such a natural response of believers wherever they are that, if they are seen, they serve as a light to the glory of God (Matthew 5:16).

A simple example of this occurred along a lengthy stretch of desert road on a hot, scorching day. The water boiled over in the car engine and we sat on the road side praying for help. Eventually a car stopped and a man got out. As soon as he saw what was wrong, he gave us water. We thanked him and referred to him as a "Good Samaritan." He responded, "Isn't that what we're all supposed to be if we follow Christ?" The stranger was a brother and one who was acting out his faith in almost unseen service. We thanked him and glorified God.

The gift of ministry is also exercised in whatever work to which one has been called. A bookkeeper exercises this gift by doing work accurately before the Lord. A businessman serves as unto the Lord, remembering that how he conducts his business will reflect upon the Lord. An employee will also do his service as unto the Lord. Whatever work a person does will speak good or ill of Christ. Wherever believers are, they are to be salt and light (Matthew 5:13-16).

The Gift of Teaching

People often limit the gift of teaching to those who are trained to expound Scripture, but it has many applications. Some who are called and gifted in teaching have a great measure of that gift along with many opportunities to instruct believers in correct doctrine. Paul charged Timothy with these words:

> I charge thee therefore before God, and the Lord Jesus Christ, who shall judge the quick and the dead at his appearing and his kingdom; Preach the word; be instant in season, out of season; reprove, rebuke, exhort with all longsuffering and doctrine. For the time will come when they will not endure sound doctrine; but after their own lusts shall they heap to themselves teachers, having itching ears; And they shall turn away their ears from the truth, and shall be turned unto fables. But watch thou in all things, endure afflictions, do the work of an evangelist, make full proof of thy ministry (2 Timothy 4:1-5).

Not only do we see how closely related teaching, preaching, and evangelizing are; we see that these activities carry a grave responsibility for keeping doctrine pure and thereby building up the saints in truth. The gift of teaching cannot be used lightly without regard to truth. Peter warns:

> But there were false prophets also among the people, even as there shall be false teachers among you, who privily shall bring in damnable heresies, even denying the Lord that bought them, and bring upon themselves swift destruction. And many shall follow their pernicious ways; by reason of whom the way of truth shall be evil spoken of. And through covetousness shall they with feigned words make merchandise of you: whose judgment now of a long time lingereth not, and their damnation slumbereth not (2 Peter 2:1-3).

While the gift of teaching may be given in greater measure to those who are especially called by God to teach the brethren, many believers exercise this gift to a lesser degree. Nevertheless, even in the seemingly smallest exercise of this gift, the believer must be sure to teach only true biblical doctrine, rather than opinions or fables, which today include all the myths created by psychological theories about who man is, why he does what he does, and how he changes.

All parents teach their children through both words and actions. Therefore, their source must also be God, for they are to exercise the gift by teaching true, biblical doctrine to their children.

While women are not to take authority over men, older women are especially instructed to teach younger women.

> The aged women likewise, that they be in behaviour as becometh holiness, not false accusers, not given to much wine, teachers of good things; That they may teach the young women to be sober, to love their husbands, to love their children, To be discreet, chaste, keepers at home, good, obedient to their own husbands, that the word of God be not blasphemed (Titus 2:3-5).

Since the Bible directs these women to teach, they will be given the necessary gift of teaching. The instruction to elder women suggests that they are teaching the younger women with their lives as well as with their words. Indeed, all believers have the opportunity to teach biblical doctrine with their own lives as they love God and obey the Word by grace through faith.

The Gift of Exhortation

The gift of exhortation is also one that may be given to a greater or lesser degree depending on the need. The Greek work *paraklesis* primarily means "a calling to one's side, and so to one's aid" and is be translated with the following words: *encouragement, exhortation, consolation, comfort.* A similar word is used in reference to the Holy Spirit in His role as Comforter. This gift is exercised when a believer comes alongside a fellow believer to encourage, exhort, console, or comfort, depending upon the need of the hour. Although the word *exhortation* is not used in Galatians 6:1-3, these verses describe how believers are to exercise that gift in restoring fellow believers.

> Brethren, if a man be overtaken in a fault, ye which are spiritual, restore such an one in the spirit of meekness; considering thyself, lest thou also be tempted. Bear ye one another's burdens, and so fulfil the law of Christ. For if a man think himself to be something, when he is nothing, he deceiveth himself.

As they come alongside a fellow believer, they may confront and exhort. They may also exercise the gift of teaching. As the sinner confesses his sin and repents, believers coming alongside will comfort and encourage. The gift of exhortation is always to be exercised in love—speaking the truth in love, "in the spirit of meekness; considering thyself, lest thou also be tempted."

Some people have a great measure of this gift operating in their lives as they come alongside to encourage. Paul exercised the gift of exhortation when he encouraged Timothy:

> When I call to remembrance the unfeigned faith that is in thee, which dwelt first in thy grandmother Lois, and thy mother Eunice; and I am persuaded that in thee also. Wherefore I put thee in remembrance that thou stir up the gift of God, which is in thee by the putting on of my hands. For God hath not given us the spirit of fear; but of power, and of love, and of a sound mind (2 Timothy 1:5-7).

Encouragement is not the same as flattery. Many people are able to say all kinds of complimentary things to their friends. But the gift of encouragement comes from God and is based on truth. Coming alongside to encourage may also be a practical action, such as helping a fellow believer with a project, making curtains for the nursery of an expectant mother, or giving any kind of aid that would speak encouragement.

The Gift of Giving

The gift of giving does not depend on one's financial ability to give large sums. All believers exercise this gift to some degree. This spiritual gift originates with God and is often an expression of gratitude and praise to God and a deep recognition that all a believer owns comes from God and rightfully belongs to God. The early believers exercised this gift when they saw fellow believers in need. They even sold their property so that no believer would be without food, clothing and shelter. "And all that believed were together, and had all things common; and sold their possessions and goods, and parted them to all men, as every man had need" (Acts 2:44-45).

The Bible tells how this gift is to be exercised. "He that giveth, let him do it with simplicity" (Romans 12:8). That means that it is to be done quietly and simply, without much ado, without special recognition, without special honor given to the giver. The gift is also to be exercised through planning, not through a sudden response to an emotional appeal: "Upon the first day of the week let every one of you lay by him in store, as God hath prospered him, that there be no gatherings when I come" (1 Corinthians 16:2). The gift is not only planned and purposeful; it is given with a godly attitude: "Every man according as he purposeth in his heart, so let him give; not grudgingly, or of necessity: for God loveth a cheerful giver" (2 Corinthians 9:7). This gift is the opposite of stealing and even an antidote to stealing: "Let him that stole steal no more: but rather let him labour, working with his hands the thing which is good, that he may have to give to him that needeth" (Ephesians 4:28).

The Gift of Ruling

The gift of ruling is an absolute necessity in the Body of Christ. One rules best who is most obedient to the Lord. This gift is one of leadership and carries grave responsibilities. Thus are added the words "with diligence." Just as a shepherd must be diligent in watching over his flock, so must leadership in the Body of Christ be exercised with great care. The gift of rulership is exercised by bishops, elders and pastors, who are to be above reproach and who already rule their own households well (1 Timothy 3:2-5; Titus 1:5-9). The gift of rulership is also given to fathers to rule their households in the Lord. This leadership is not only to be with words, but also by example. Peter exhorts the elders:

> Feed the flock of God which is among you, taking the oversight thereof, not by constraint, but willingly; not for filthy lucre, but of a ready mind; Neither as being lords over God's heritage, but being ensamples to the flock. And when the chief Shepherd shall appear, ye shall receive a crown of glory that fadeth not away (1 Peter 5:2-4).

Rulers in the household of faith carry a heavy weight of responsibility for the believers under their care. Therefore, James says:

> My brethren, be not many masters, knowing that we shall receive the greater condemnation. For in many things we offend all. If any man offend not in word, the same is a perfect man, and able also to bridle the whole body (James 3:1-2).

Those who lead must, therefore, lead according to the gift of rulership given by the grace of God and exercised through faith and in love and humility.

Some people confuse ministry and leadership. They assume that leaders are to perform the bulk of the ministry. Some pastors are expected to teach and preach Sunday morning, evangelize Sunday evening, teach the mid-week Bible study, lead the singing, preside at every meeting, clean the church, cut the grass, call on every-one who is sick, personally minister to all who are dis-tressed, and be available to every member at all times. No wonder some pastors have punted to psychothera-pists!

Leaders are to lead and participate as examples, but the bulk of ministry is the responsibility of the rest of the Body. While not everyone is called and equipped for leadership positions, all—from babes in Christ to mature believers—are called and equipped to serve God and minister to one another by grace through faith.

The Gift of Showing Mercy

Showing mercy is another gift distributed through-out the Body and exercised in various ways both through words and actions. It is noteworthy that mercy is to be exercised "with cheerfulness." Mercy has and shows compassion. This gift operates through acts of kindness and assistance to those in need. This gift will succor the receiver of care without making him feel worthless or an object of pity. Compassion can also be expressed simply through listening and conversing. Mercy is further expressed through patience and long-suffering, through overlooking the faults of others, and through forgiveness.

Comfort is often given simply by one's presence and availability during a difficult trial. In this way the gifts of ministry and exhortation come together. Too often we think of these gifts only operating through the spoken word, when more often than anyone realizes these gifts operate through actions. When a woman heard that her friend's child had died, she went to be with her. Later the bereaved mother told the woman how much it meant just to have her there with her. She said that what she appreciated most was her friend's quiet pres-ence. Not many words were spoken. The comfort came simply from her sister in Christ coming alongside, being ready to listen, to care, to love, to pray, and to weep with those who weep. Too often people think they must talk to make others feel better. Instead, there was time for quiet reflection and mutual understanding together in the presence of the Lord, who is the "God of all comfort" (2 Corinthians 1:3). Here even the actions were simple expressions of love—a cup of tea, a hand clasp, a coming alongside.

God Distributes the Gifts

Some people mistakenly categorize people according to a psychological understanding of these gifts as categories that match traits and temperaments. Then by administering a type of Spiritual Gift Inventory they line up interests and traits with the various gifts and then assign certain gifts to individuals according to gift categories. A person may then be identified according to a gift category, such as being called a "mercy person" with the gift of mercy. Then follows a description of this type of person with so-called strengths and weakness. While the alleged purpose is to help people identify their gifts so that they can have confidence to minister, such inventories are fleshly devices similar to personality tests. Such tests are not valid. Moreover, such tests and inventories appeal to the flesh, disregard the manner in which the Lord may distribute the gifts, and often limit individuals in their service to the Lord. Just think what might have happened if Stephen had taken a Spiritual Gift Inventory and learned that his gift was administration—to oversee the serving at tables. He no doubt would have lived longer. But, instead of being limited by having been assigned a gift of administration, Stephen followed the Holy Spirit as opportunity was given. In his defense before the religious leaders, he presented a powerful testimony of God's dealings with Israel. For this he was stoned, but there was much fruit to the glory of God (Acts 7).

Rather than assigning gifts to individuals through a Spiritual Gift Inventory, Christians must realize that it is God who distributes the gifts according to the need of the Body and by His own good pleasure. Although the gifts are exercised by individual members, the gifts are given to the entire Body. Individual persons do not own the gifts they exercise by God's grace. God distributes gifts for ministry for His purpose. "Every good gift and every perfect gift is from above, and cometh down from the Father of lights, with whom is no variableness, neither shadow of turning" (James 1:17).

Every gift of ministry comes from God and operates by faith. Every gift is exercised for fruitfulness in the Lord and should be accompanied by the fruit of the Spirit: "love, joy, peace, longsuffering, gentleness, goodness, faith, meekness, temperance" (Galatians 5:22,23). Love is the basis for all ministry. Notice how this love is to be expressed through attitudes and actions as well as through words:

> Let love be without dissimulation. Abhor that which is evil; cleave to that which is good. Be kindly affectioned one to another with brotherly love; in honour preferring one another; Not slothful in business; fervent in spirit; serving the Lord; Rejoicing in hope; patient in tribulation; continuing instant in prayer; Distributing to the necessity of saints; given to hospitality. Bless them which persecute you: bless, and curse not. Rejoice with them that do rejoice, and weep with them that weep. Be of the same mind one toward another. Mind not high things, but condescend to men of low estate. Be not wise in your own conceits (Romans 12:9-16).

Truly, if believers were to take these verses seriously in their relationships with one another, the Body of Christ would be edified in love and there would be eternal fruit! Indeed, every believer is called, gifted, equipped and competent to serve. Mutual care in the Body of Christ is a high calling, but it is a calling common to every member.

5

Caring for Souls Inside and Out

The primary care of souls is accomplished by God. He is the one who both saves and sanctifies. Nevertheless He involves His children through gifts of ministry to the church and through the mutual care of believers in the Body of Christ. Because the care of souls involves both the inner and outer aspects of the individual, there have been different approaches and emphases through the centuries. Some have focused on external behavior and primarily dealt directly with external sin. Others have sought to investigate the inner workings of the soul.

Jesus teaches about the inner sinfulness of those who may obey external laws, but who harbor the root of sin in their hearts. He says:

> Ye have heard that it was said by them of old time,
> Thou shalt not kill; and whosoever shall kill shall
> be in danger of the judgment: But I say unto you,
> That whosoever is angry with his brother without
> a cause shall be in danger of the judgment. . .
> (Matthew 5:21-22).

Jesus further declares:

> Ye have heard that it was said by them of old time,
> Thou shalt not commit adultery: But I say unto
> you, That whosoever looketh on a woman to lust
> after her hath committed adultery with her
> already in his heart (Matthew 5:27-28).

The Pharisees, who were very concerned about outward appearances of righteousness, complained to
Jesus about His disciples eating without washing their
hands. In response to such concerns, Jesus teaches that
the source of sinful attitudes and actions is the heart:

> And he saith unto them, Are ye so without under-
> standing also? Do ye not perceive, that whatsoever
> thing from without entereth into the man, it can-
> not defile him; Because it entereth not into his
> heart, but into the belly, and goeth out into the
> draught, purging all meats? And he said, That
> which cometh out of the man, that defileth the
> man. For from within, out of the heart of men,
> proceed evil thoughts, adulteries, fornications,
> murders, thefts, covetousness, wickedness, deceit,
> lasciviousness, an evil eye, blasphemy, pride, fool-
> ishness: All these evil things come from within,
> and defile the man (Mark 7:18-23).

Because "evil thoughts, adulteries, fornications,
murders, thefts, covetousness, wickedness, deceit,
lasciviousness, an evil eye, blasphemy, pride, foolish-
ness," and all other sinful expressions come from the
heart, the care of souls cannot overlook the inner person
and concern itself with external behavior only. The

question is, however, what is the human participation
in the care of souls? What is God's part and what can be
ministered by and through fellow believers?

Salvation is an inner work of God which leads to
actions. Paul says:

> For by grace are ye saved through faith; and that
> not of yourselves: it is the gift of God: Not of
> works, lest any man should boast. For we are his
> workmanship, created in Christ Jesus unto good
> works, which God hath before ordained that we
> should walk in them (Ephesians 2:8-10).

Here is the inner work of God resulting in good works,
which include both internal and external activity. Elsewhere Paul writes:

> But the righteousness which is of faith speaketh
> on this wise, Say not in thine heart, Who shall
> ascend into heaven? (that is, to bring Christ down
> from above:) Or, Who shall descend into the deep?
> (that is, to bring up Christ again from the dead.)
> But what saith it? The word is nigh thee, even in
> thy mouth, and in thy heart: that is, the word of
> faith, which we preach; That if thou shalt confess
> with thy mouth the Lord Jesus, and shalt believe
> in thine heart that God hath raised him from the
> dead, thou shalt be saved. For with the heart man
> believeth unto righteousness; and with the mouth
> confession is made unto salvation (Romans 10:6-
> 10).

Again we see the inner work of faith and the outward
expression of confession "made unto salvation."

However, there is also human involvement in
preaching the Good News of salvation, for the Word
says:

> For whosoever shall call upon the name of the
> Lord shall be saved. How then shall they call on
> him in whom they have not believed? and how

shall they believe in him of whom they have not
heard? and how shall they hear without a
preacher? And how shall they preach, except they
be sent? as it is written, How beautiful are the
feet of them that preach the gospel of peace, and
bring glad tidings of good things! (Romans 10:13-
15).

The Lord uses the human instrument of preaching to
accomplish His work within the hearer. The preacher
ministers to the inner person through the Word of God,
but God accomplishes that inner work.

The Bible and Human Complexities

The Bible speaks to the whole person both individually and within society. The Bible speaks to one's inner-
most being, including the mind, heart, soul, and all that
is nonphysical—the spirit or psyche. The Bible also
addresses the external behavior of the individual, both
as the manifestation of the inner life and within the
context of other people and external circumstances. In
other words, the Bible addresses the entire human
condition.

Moreover, the Bible addresses the human condition
in relation to God and reveals two kinds of humans, the
first being only a descendent of Adam and the second
having been born again by the Spirit (Romans 5, 6).
Those who have been born of God are indwelt by the
Spirit and are even more complex than unbelievers. Not
only do they have an inner life and an external life exercised individually and socially; Christ is the essence of
their new inner life, and their external life is more and
more to reflect His life. Moreover, Christians have a
new relationship to other people in that they are now
intrinsically related to other members of the Body of
Christ, which is made up of all those who are born
again.

Such complexity of each individual believer could be
mind boggling, especially since each one experiences

different circumstances. The complexity expands as we consider Romans 8:28-29:

> And we know that all things work together for good to them that love God, to them who are the called according to his purpose. For whom he did foreknow, he also did predestinate to be conformed to the image of his Son, that he might be the first-born among many brethren.

What astonishing creativity! God works all things together to conform each of His children "to the image of his Son"! Taking this verse literally means that every word spoken, every situation, every detail of each believer's life is being "worked together" by God for His purpose. He is the Creator and He is the One who conforms believers to the image of His Son. He does all this, with each one, while He allows each to make various choices. He does all of this without turning anyone into a puppet.

Considering that Christians "are his workmanship, created in Christ Jesus unto good works, which God hath before ordained that we should walk in them" (Ephesians 2:10), why must they look to outside systems to help believers in their walk with the Lord? Why are so many people who call themselves "Christian psychologists" or even "biblical counselors" attempting to peer inside Christians to analyze their psyche or identify specific "idols of the heart" and thereby bring about change? They may indeed be attempting to do what only God can do and thereby trespassing in places where only God is able to walk.

Christians are too complex to analyze. They cannot remake themselves or each other. God does the inner work. The Holy Spirit brings conviction to the heart. God's Word also does the inner work:

> For the Word of God is quick, and powerful, and sharper than any twoedged sword, piercing even to the dividing asunder of soul and spirit, and of

the joints and marrow, and is a discerner of the thoughts and intents of the heart. Neither is there any creature that is not manifest in his sight: but all things are naked and opened unto the eyes of him with whom we have to do (Hebrews 4:12).

David looked to God to search his heart and bring correction when he prayed:

Search me, O God, and know my heart: try me, and know my thoughts: And see if there be any wicked way in me, and lead me in the way everlasting (Psalms 139:23,24).

There are numerous ways believers can minister to one another in the care of souls ministry, but the inside work is God's work within an individual believer and that believer's inner response to God.

Not even Paul tried to analyze individual believers. Yet he ministered to the inner person. He taught people. He exhorted and rebuked them. He encouraged them. He trusted God for the inner work, as he explained how believers work out what God works within them.

Wherefore, my beloved, as ye have always obeyed, not as in my presence only, but now much more in my absence, work out your own salvation with fear and trembling. For it is God which worketh in you both to will and to do of his good pleasure (Philippians 2:12,13).

God does the inside work. Each believer works out what God is working in him both individually and as a member of Christ's Body.

As God's Word is read, as doctrines are taught and learned, as teachers exegete Scripture, as fellow believers testify of Christ and live the Christian life in close proximity to other believers, the Word is planted in hearts and the water of life brings growth. But, it is God who brings the increase. It is God at work behind the scenes, within the heart, within the mind. Believers may exhort, may come alongside speaking the truth in love, but they need not analyze the soul, nor should they. The inner work is God's work within a believer. He may use a word spoken by a brand new believer instead of wisdom from one mature in the faith. He may use a child's question rather than an adult's answer to turn a wayward soul back to Himself.

All this business of trying to develop a counseling system that addresses the vast complexity of a believer's life within the Body of Christ is usually a waste of time. If secular notions about the psyche and how to help people change are integrated, recycled or embraced in any way, it is worse than time wasted. It is idolatry! It is looking to something other than what God has already provided in Himself, through His Word, His Son, the Holy Spirit, and Christ's Body. If people are not being changed into the likeness of Christ by what God has already given, why do human beings suppose they can do any better? Do they presume to develop a better plan by looking at the notions of unsaved men who have supposedly studied the psyche?

The best counsel anyone can give or receive originates from Scripture, focuses on Christ, and encourages a person to trust and obey God. One does not have to analyze a psyche, nor should one even try. Neither must one become an "expert" of the soul, nor can he. One does not have to be a Bible scholar with a wall covered with certificates and degrees to minister God's grace. One only needs to know Christ and to be walking according to the Spirit.

Idols of the Heart

There are those in the church who believe that ministry occurs on various levels from the superficial to that which reaches deeply into a person's soul. They suggest that to engage in the deepest level of ministry, one must be able to understand the intricacies of the soul through some form of enlightenment. Many have turned to psychoanalytic theories of the unconscious for such insight. Others have turned back to what the Puritans were attempting to accomplish by analyzing the soul and revealing the "idols of the heart."

The designation "idols of the heart" comes from Scripture, particularly as recorded by Ezekiel:

> And the word of the LORD came unto me, saying, Son of man, these men have set up their idols in their heart, and put the stumblingblock of their iniquity before their face: should I be inquired of at all by them? Therefore speak unto them, and say unto them, Thus saith the Lord GOD; Every man of the house of Israel that setteth up his idols in his heart, and putteth the stumblingblock of his iniquity before his face, and cometh to the prophet; I the LORD will answer him that cometh according to the multitude of his idols; That I may take the house of Israel in their own heart, because they are all estranged from me through their idols. Therefore say unto the house of Israel, Thus saith the Lord GOD; Repent, and turn yourselves from your idols; and turn away your faces from all your abominations (Ezekiel 14:2-6).

Indeed all true idolatry begins inside a person. It involves more than external idols, such as those made of wood or stone. Idolatry puts something or someone else in God's place.

The nations around Israel worshipped idols. They prayed, burned incense, and sacrificed to them in order to improve their lives. Sacrifices were made for fertility and fruitfulness, for victories and plunder. An idol has always been anything a person trusts for help instead of God. If he trusts in that idol, he will worship and sacrifice and do according to what he believes the idol wants. The more devoted one is to an idol and the more faith and trust invested in an idol, the more that idol becomes an idol of the heart.

In our era we have our own set of idolatries, all of which consist of loving the world more than loving God.

> Love not the world, neither the things that are in the world. If any man love the world, the love of the Father is not in him. For all that is in the world, the lust of the flesh, and the lust of the eyes, and the pride of life, is not of the Father, but is of the world. And the world passeth away, and the lust thereof: but he that doeth the will of God abideth for ever (1 John 2:15-17).

Anything in the world or in the world's systems can become an idol of the heart.

The Reformers considered all disobedience to God to be idolatry of the heart. Puritan ministers had a keen interest in identifying idols of the heart. They desired to be holy and to make all believers under their care holy. It was not enough for them to get rid of external sin. They believed it was their duty to cure hearts by getting rid of the idols. To do so, they would spend much time examining the spiritual condition of individual souls. Through various questions they attempted to discover whether an individual was indeed saved. Then they would seek to uncover secret sins and expose the idols of the heart. Some even thought they could chart the progression of each person's soul and determine which point along the way to maturity the person had reached. In his book titled *A History of Pastoral Care in America: From Salvation to Self-Realization*, E. Brooks Holifield says:

> Pious New Englanders, especially, wanted to learn how to map their progress, and the Puritan pastors became masters of introspection, cartographers of the inner life, adept at recognizing the signs of salvation.[1]

In their zeal for holiness, they sought to go right to the core, to those inner depths of the soul.

> The Puritan pastor, especially in the seventeenth century, became a specialist in the cure of the idolatrous heart. He analyzed motives, evaluated feel-

ings, sought to discern hidden intentions and to direct inward consent.[2]

But for such analysis they needed to speculate about how the mind worked, how the will could be turned, and what might be the relationship of reason, emotion, understanding, and the will. With all their expertise they could not see inside another person. They may have thought they were successful in uncovering hidden sin and in some instances they may have been correct because of external manifestations (sinful behavior that could be observed) of a particular heart idol.

One can imagine the interrogation, the suspicion, if you please, the discomfort, the suggestions, the accusations, the dissent, and, alas, the acquiescence to confessing inward sin not revealed by the Holy Spirit, but imposed by those who were eager to make people holy. What could an ordinary Christian do but agree with the one who was superior in education and position? Since Christians of that day expected their pastors to be able to understand, interpret, and analyze the intricacies of the soul, what could anyone do but accept whatever spiritual diagnosis might be given?

But what concerns us most is that to look inside another person, a pastor had to go outside Scripture. He had to make assumptions about the mind, the heart, and the will. But the only mind, heart, and will with which he was familiar was his own. Even here, he could not be sure, because of the possible self-deception of a heart that is deceitful. In fact the Bible verse that speaks of the deceitful heart reveals that those holy, well-meaning men were trying to do what only God could do:

> The heart is deceitful above all things, and desperately wicked: who can know it? I the LORD search the heart, I try the reins, even to give every man according to his ways, and according to the fruit of his doings (Jeremiah 17:9,10).

While the desire to guide people in their walk with the Lord was admirable, there is a subtle danger when one person tries to look inside another to determine that individual's idols of the heart. The Puritan focus on the soul's interior life could easily lead to self-absorption and introspection. As one looks at the history of theology and pastoral care, one can see the Puritan's contribution to a growing fascination with the self and the later integration of secular psychological therapies and their underlying psychologies. Regarding the connection between the Puritans and psychology Holifield says:

> American pastoral care traditions are rooted in an ancient introspective piety which demands that Christian clergy possess a knowledge of the inner world. It would not be outrageous to suggest that the extraordinary preoccupation with psychology in twentieth-century America owes something to the heritage of experiential piety; that America became a nation of psychologists in part because it had once been a land of Pietists.[3]

Not only did this country become *The Psychological Society*,[4] the church itself is now infected with that kind of psychology. Moreover, members of the very movement that has been working to provide biblical counsel in place of psychological counseling are becoming more and more fascinated with the inner life and seeking to uncover the idols of the heart as did their Puritan forefathers. But doing so creates the soil for the subtleties of psychology to come in and contaminate what is intended to be pure.

Besides preparing the way for psychotherapy, the Puritans failed to emphasize evangelism and mutual care in the Body of Christ. The Puritan pastor was the "expert" of the soul and the Puritan was intensely occupied with the condition of his own soul. In "Perils of Puritanism," Thomas N. Smith says:

The pull of such individualism and subjectivity in Christian experience and ethics is away from, rather than toward the church, as the body of Christ. Thus, there is little emphasis in the Puritans on the role of the church as a fellowship of real Christians met together for worship and mutual edification.[5]

Christians can learn much from the Puritans' zeal to live godly lives, but need to beware of the pull of the flesh towards subjectivity, introspection, and reliance on "experts" of the soul. Rather than looking at their own selves, believers are called to look out for the welfare of others. We have a mandate from God to love one another and serve one another in the Body of Christ. We also have a mandate to reach out to evangelize the lost. The church has moved off track by emphasizing the process of counseling with its subjectivity, speculation about the psyche, and penchant to peer into another person's heart.

In seeking to expand biblical counseling beyond the external and visible behavior and beyond the activities provided by Scripture, there are biblical counselors who are eager to explore the inner man and thereby to gain and use special knowledge. Not satisfied with simply confronting individuals regarding behavior they can observe, they want to delve into the inner workings of the heart and thereby discern and judge motivation. Like the Puritans, they are working to become specialists in curing the idolatrous heart by evaluating feelings and analyzing motives.

Although biblical counselors recognize many contradictions, failures, and false promises and premises of the psychological way, many continue to use portions of various psychological theories and therapies they think agree with Scripture. The practice of attempting to understand another person's soul and to identify that person's "idols of the heart" closely parallels various forms of psychological analysis. However, the very process of analysis is nonbiblical and should not be practiced. Just because one uses Bible verses, biblical terminology, and biblical goals for change does not make analyzing the soul biblical. That is because analysis works at cross purposes to the Holy Spirit, who does not have to analyze a person in order to identify the idols of the heart. But, since our nation has been raised on psychoanalytic assumptions, most assume that analyzing one's actions, thoughts, and motives will lead to understanding the self or the soul and thereby help one change.

The deception is similar to a Gnostic mentality—that knowledge will bring change. But, how many times does one know better but fail to do better? Understanding one's own self through any kind of prolonged analysis may help one change some thoughts and actions, but it may also increase self-absorption and self-deception, for the soul can only be known and understood by God. Far better than speculating about the idols of the heart would be focusing on Christ, abiding in Christ, believing His Word, and following biblical rather than psychological or analytical means for change.

Those who call themselves biblical counselors and who specialize in identifying the idols of the heart have had to dip into the psychological theories of the world. The Bible clearly identifies sin, and the Holy Spirit reveals the idols of one's own heart. However, the Bible does not instruct anyone to look into another person's soul to identify or analyze that person's idols of the heart. One must go outside Scripture to do what the Bible does not teach. This idols-of-the-heart methodology can be a serious impediment to true ministry. The notion that one must be able to identify the idols of another person's heart may intimidate and thereby discourage believers from ministering to one another. Moreover, counsel based on speculation about another person's inner life may sorely mislead a fellow believer who is being treated as a "counselee" and analyzed by a "counselor."

We cannot identify the idols residing in another person's heart, but we can see evidence of what people trust. We can certainly see evidence of one of the greatest idolatries in the church today—the idolatry of psychology. Rather than looking to God for personal growth and for solving problems of living, Christians are looking to the made-made creations of psychology. The kind of psychology they turn to is not even science. It is a conglomeration of notions concocted by those who rejected God and formed their own theories about who man is and how he is to change and grow. This kind of psychology is religion rather than science. It is a false religion in place of God. Because psychological counseling theories and therapies constitute another religion they must attempt to do what God does. They must attempt to look into the soul, analyze it, and change a person from the inside out, or as with the behaviorists, they attempt to reach and change the soul through outside forces, such as operant conditioning.

Those who promote counseling in which the counselor is probing for the idols in the heart of the one being counseled are similar to Job's counselors, who were convinced that Job was being punished by God for hidden sins. They tried to get at those sins through much idle speculation and accusation. They were troublesome instead of helpful, because they had an agenda—to discover Job's hidden sin to make him confess before them and before God to end Job's punishment. Job's arguments to them would be seen as denial and self-protective strategies if he were being counseled by some who call themselves biblical counselors today.

Some important lessons in Job have to do with the sovereignty of God, the faithfulness of God, and the sufficiency of God. God had allowed difficult circumstances for His own purpose, but, because Job's counselors relied on their own wisdom and legalistic view of God, they sinned against Job and against God. Had they just sat with Job, avoided idle speculation, and never opened their mouths, they would have been the wiser.

But, in their pride and self-righteousness, they presumed to know what they did not know, and they had the audacity of attempting to pry into Job's inner man and of making false accusations.

Caring for Souls Inside and Out

The care of souls does involve the inner person. The care of souls does address and attack the idols of the heart. But such work is **not** done by "counselors" analyzing another person's inner life. What we can do for each other in the care of souls continues to be what is given throughout the New Testament. We can teach, preach, testify, exhort, encourage, come alongside, speak the truth in love, rebuke, identify external sin, correct, comfort, forgive, and pray. These activities minister to the inner and outer person.

Humans may guess at the idols of another person's heart by observing external sin, but, even with external evidence, they may be drawing the wrong conclusions. If there is sin, there is an idol of the heart; there is love of the world manifesting itself in "the lust of the flesh, and the lust of the eyes, and the pride of life." But, the way out is not through one person, called "counselor," peering inside the psyche of another person, called "counselee," to identify and analyze. True change is brought about by God working in the individual. As He is doing something miraculous in a believer's heart, He uses the external efforts of believers teaching, preaching, testifying, exhorting, encouraging, coming alongside, speaking the truth in love, identifying external sin, rebuking, correcting, comforting, forgiving, praying, helping in practical matters of life, and being a living example of walking in the Spirit. We are not left with superficial, external help. Instead, God calls us to minister to one another on the human level while He accomplishes the miraculous inner work on the soul.

> For though we walk in the flesh, we do not war after the flesh: (For the weapons of our warfare

are not carnal, but mighty through God to the pulling down of strong holds;) Casting down imaginations, and every high thing that exalteth itself against the knowledge of God, and bringing into captivity every thought to the obedience of Christ (2 Corinthians 10:3-5).

6

The Whole Counsel of God

When Jesus was tempted in the wilderness, He declared: "It is written, Man shall not live by bread alone, but by every word that proceedeth out of the mouth of God" (Matthew 4:4). Jesus taught truth that would set people free. His words are as applicable today as the day He promised: "If ye continue in my word, then are ye my disciples indeed; And ye shall know the truth, and the truth shall make you free" (John 8:31,32). Jesus continues to teach truth through His Word. But for one to know the truth and to be set free by the truth, one must continue in it. What does that mean?

As important as reading and studying the Bible are, the essence of what Jesus is saying is that those who continue in His Word by doing it are the ones who both know truth and are set free by truth. The word translated "continue" can also be translated "abide" or "remain." If one hears the Word and does not obey the Word, he is not continuing, abiding or remaining in the Word. Jesus is talking about following what He says and living accordingly.

Jesus' well-known story about the man who built his house on the rock in contrast to the one who built his house on the sand (Matthew 7:24-27) illustrates the vast difference between the one who hears and obeys the Word and those who hear but do not obey. As important as hearing and reading the Word of God are, the benefit comes from responding in faith and obedience.

There are some believers who follow the Lord, but only to a point. They may carefully avoid certain sins but disregard the rest of God's counsel. However, Jesus calls His followers into such a close relationship with Himself that He abides in them and they abide in Him. As they mature as believers, they will more and more continue, remain, and abide in the whole counsel of God. Even new believers, who are just beginning to abide in Christ, are enabled both to obey and to minister to one another through obedience to what they know of God's Word.

We want to encourage Christians to continue learning and studying God's Word, just as Paul encouraged Timothy:

> Study to show thyself approved unto God, a workman that needeth not to be ashamed, rightly dividing the word of truth. But shun profane and vain babblings: for they will increase unto more ungodliness (2 Timothy 2:15,16).

The more believers read, study, learn, think about, and obey God's Word, the better equipped they are to minister to fellow believers. Yet, believers can serve along the way even before they have learned a great deal of Scripture. For instance, Jesus commended a Roman centurion for his faith.

> And when Jesus was entered into Capernaum, there came unto him a centurion, beseeching him, And saying, Lord, my servant lieth at home sick of the palsy, grievously tormented. And Jesus saith unto him, I will come and heal him.
>
> The centurion answered and said, Lord, I am not worthy that thou shouldest come under my roof: but speak the word only, and my servant shall be healed. For I am a man under authority, having soldiers under me: and I say to this man, Go, and he goeth; and to another, Come, and he cometh; and to my servant, Do this, and he doeth it.
>
> When Jesus heard it, he marvelled, and said to them that followed, Verily I say unto you, I have not found so great faith, no, not in Israel (Matthew 8:5-10).

The centurion had heard Jesus teach, but he had probably never read a word of Scripture. He believed what Jesus said and he acted accordingly. He was serving God by faith at an early stage of learning. Believers can and should begin acting and serving by faith from the very beginning of their new life in Him.

Notice the centurion's humility. He said, "Lord, I am not worthy that thou shouldest come under my roof: but speak the word only, and my servant shall be healed." Without humility and a teachable attitude, one may read the Word with some intellectual comprehension but without spiritual apprehension. An English professor at a nearby university, who taught the Bible as literature, had the reputation of putting the Bible on the floor and stomping on it to demonstrate that it was just a book made of paper, glue, and ink. Yes, he could point out literary features. Although he taught the Bible, he did not have ears to hear the message of salvation.

Some people are able to apply the Word to other people, but fail to see their own failings. Pride is a main detriment to receiving and obeying the Word of God. But, when a person comes to know and love the Savior, he will be eager to learn and be transformed by the Word. The Lord will work humility and meekness into the person's life as a gardener softens the soil. The more the person then abides in the Word and the more the person learns that he cannot do anything apart from abiding in Christ, the fruit of meekness and humility will increase and he will be even more receptive to the Word and the work of the Holy Spirit in his life.

The Word of God and the Holy Spirit work together to establish believers in truth and to mature and equip believers for life and service. The Word is preeminent— to be read, studied, learned, preached, taught, followed, obeyed, and kept. Paul wrote:

> For this cause also thank we God without ceasing, because, when ye received the word of God which ye heard of us, ye received it not as the word of men, but as it is in truth, the word of God, which effectually worketh also in you that believe (1 Thessalonians 2:13).

As believers continue in the Word, they know the truth and are set free from sin and self. They are set free to serve God. Whenever a believer experiences problems of living he should seek wisdom and truth from God's Word rather than worldly counsel. Then he will receive from the Lord and be further equipped to minister God's grace to fellow believers.

Finding God in His Word

Seeking the wisdom and counsel of God when over-come by problems need not be a frantic search for specific verses or quick remedies. What a believer must seek is God Himself through His Word. Because of God's presence in a believer's life and the activity of the Holy Spirit in relation to God's Word, the Word works super-naturally in him. The first work of the Word is to remind the believer about who God is and about his relationship to God through faith. The Word will engen-der faith, peace, and the inner resources necessary for dealing with problems of living. Through the Word and the work of the Holy Spirit, God will conform the believer into the image of Christ in the midst of problems. As believers draw close to God during difficult times they can say with Paul:

> Therefore being justified by faith, we have peace with God through our Lord Jesus Christ: By whom also we have access by faith into this grace wherein we stand, and rejoice in hope of the glory of God. And not only so, but we glory in tribulations also: knowing that tribulation worketh patience; and patience, experience; and experience, hope: and hope maketh not ashamed; because the love of God is shed abroad in our hearts by the Holy Ghost which is given unto us (Romans 5:1-5).

Numerous people have testified about knowing God better through life's extremities. Scripture that is believed by faith and followed by God's enabling truly ministers help in time of need. As believers learn this through their own experience, they are able to encourage others as well. Even fairly new believers who have found God sufficient in the midst of problems know:

> There hath no temptation taken you but such as is common to man: but God is faithful, who will not suffer you to be tempted above that ye are able; but will with the temptation also make a way to escape, that ye may be able to bear it (1 Corinthians 10:13).

All believers who have found God faithful to this Scripture can minister effectively in encouraging fellow believers to trust God in the midst of problems. One does not have to know the entire Bible to minister the truth of the Word that has been understood, applied, and obeyed. The Scriptures that truly set people free are those that have been followed on a regular basis. The more one lives Scripture, the more he can be used by God. If one truly knew and lived one Scripture (e.g.

Matthew 16:24-27), one would be more mature than those who know hundreds of Scriptures but live none.

Moving Away from Problem-Centered Counseling

People generally seek counseling to deal with problems of living. Counseling very naturally becomes problem-centered. Some forms of counseling attempt to analyze the self or the soul to discover the roots of the problems. Other forms attempt to help individuals change their thinking and behaving more directly. All seem to focus on problems, even when personal or spiritual growth is the final goal.

While there are times when problems of living may be solved directly through exhortation and through applying specific verses that relate directly to those problems, we contend that personal ministry should move away from problems. By saying this we do not mean that we overlook problems or merely sweep them aside. If there is known sin to confess, if there is restitution to be made, if there are necessary changes, these should be done according to biblical means of spiritual sanctification. The Lord may use His Word directly to the individual who is in need, or the Holy Spirit may convict the soul while the person is listening to a sound preacher exegete Scripture, or a fellow believer may say a word that edifies, encourages or exhorts. As a person hears and responds to the Word of God and the work of the Holy Spirit, he will grow. The Holy Spirit will both convict of sin and work the necessary change.

While problem-centered counseling may use certain Scriptures that seem appropriate, the focus is wrong. Christians grow and change as they look at Christ, not as they analyze their problems or feelings. Endless talk about personal problems and feelings encourages self-focus. There are some people who actually enjoy the attention they receive in a problem-centered environment. As long as they continue to have problems or overcome problems they are center stage. Often such people persist in their problems. While they may overcome some problems along the way, there may be very little spiritual growth. A friend refers to these people as "crisis-centered instead of Christ-centered."

Those who want to care for souls often believe that they must have a manual or other or book of verses listed according to problems so that they will have the "right" verses to give those suffering from problems of living. They think they must be trained in biblical counseling so that they will be able to connect specific verses to specific problems. Without this special training they feel inadequate. But, do they really need to know how to treat problems with specific verses? What if the person has a multitude of problems and all the time is spent putting out fires with spurts of out-of-context verses when the person really needs to know God and begin to trust Him in the midst of problems?

A person who has not been trained in "counseling" may actually depend more fully on the Lord than one who has a credential and a manual. The person who does "not know how" to deal with specific problems with specific verses may simply pray with the person, read and study Scripture with the person, and seek God together with the person for His perfect will to be done. We want to encourage believers to permit the Holy Spirit to use what they have already learned from Scripture as they care for souls. Every believer who has studied and obeyed the Word has a storehouse of Scripture ready to be used by the Spirit in ministering to the one who needs help. The believer who uses what he has learned and obeyed and who trusts God has much to minister to a struggling soul.

People who engage in problem-centered counseling assume that as people learn verses and work on specific problems of living, spiritual growth will occur. However, that does not necessarily follow. The Bible emphasizes knowing and loving God and His Word, walking according to the Spirit, growing in the fruit of the Spirit, and loving one another as Christ loves us. Instead of focusing on problems in a counseling setting, believers should look to the Lord and increase their knowledge of Him. "But we all, with open face beholding as in a glass the glory of the Lord, are changed into the same image from glory to glory, even as by the Spirit of the Lord" (2 Corinthians 3:18).

While the Lord may use pastors, teachers, and fellow believers to give comfort, encouragement, and wise counsel in time of need, believers are instructed to come directly to Christ. There they will find wisdom, guidance, strength, and love through His Word and the Holy Spirit. The Lord uses difficulties to conform believers to the image of Christ. If believers focus on overcoming problems of living more than on the Lord, they may miss what God is doing and wants to do. If they focus on problems and even on specific verses that seem to fit those problems, they may attempt to manipulate or to get their own way or avoid the inner work that must be done in their souls by the Word and the Holy Spirit. Finally, problem-centered counseling may help individuals strengthen their flesh rather than strengthen their spiritual walk in the Lord.

The Whole Counsel of God

Rather than identifying specific verses and using them for specific problems without connecting those verses with the rest of the Bible, a believer needs to come under the authority, guidance, scrutiny, and power of the whole counsel of God. The whole counsel of God is what the Bible says in the context of its entirety. While believers may turn to and refer to specific verses to determine what God has said, those verses are to be understood by the rest of the Bible. A verse is understood on the basis not only of the immediate context of the verses surrounding it, but in the context of the entire Bible. Otherwise there is danger of legalism devoid of grace, on the one hand, and the danger of mercy without truth, on the other, with a multitude of other possible misinterpretations and misguidance. Biblical doctrines are consistent with all of the Bible.

The Bible is the place where Christians are meant to live, not just visit. People become familiar with their own homes. They know what's there and what isn't. They move from room to room with ease and find comfort and solace. They know where the refrigerator is and they may even remember its contents. They are "at home" at home. That is a crude analogy for spending time in the Word, finding nourishment from the Word, and resting in the Word.

Jesus teaches believers that His Words are to abide in them. The believer is not only to become familiar with the Word, but to ingest and digest the Word to the degree that it permeates his entire being. Just as food nourishes every cell of the body, God's Word is meant to nourish every iota of the inner man. Jesus resisted Satan's temptation in the wilderness with these words: "Man shall not live by bread alone, but by every word that proceedeth out of the mouth of God" (Matthew 4:4). God's Word is the sustenance of the believer.

Believers would do well to read and study the entire Bible. Those who teach the Bible should study and teach portions of Scripture in the context of the entire Bible. But, believers do not have to know the entire Bible before they begin to minister to one another in the Body of Christ for three reasons: (1) the supernatural essence of Scripture, (2) the Holy Spirit's presence, (3) the way the Scriptures are organized. The earlier example of the person who only recited John 3:16 reveals the supernatural essence of Scripture, the work of the Holy Spirit drawing the listener to Himself, the amount of doctrine compressed into that one verse, and how God can use even a babe in Christ.

The Supernatural Word of God

Scripture is supernatural both in that it is God-breathed and that it accomplishes its intended goal. Scripture is not simply man's ideas about God and about how to live. The Bible is the very Word of God given by inspiration to humans to record.

> Knowing this first, that no prophecy of the scripture is of any private interpretation. For the prophecy came not in old time by the will of man: but holy men of God spake as they were moved by the Holy Ghost (2 Peter 1:20,21).

People were not simply inspired by thoughts about God. The words of the Bible came from God Himself. Note what Scripture accomplishes in the following verses:

> But continue thou in the things which thou hast learned and hast been assured of, knowing of whom thou hast learned them; And that from a child thou hast known the holy scriptures, which are able to make thee wise unto salvation through faith which is in Christ Jesus.
>
> All scripture is given by inspiration of God, and is profitable for doctrine, for reproof, for correction, for instruction in righteousness: That the man of God may be perfect, thoroughly furnished unto all good works (2 Timothy 3:14-17).

Scripture is supernatural in its origin and its work to make one "wise unto salvation through faith which is in Christ Jesus"; is "profitable for doctrine, for reproof, for correction, for instruction in righteousness"; and brings a believer to maturity and equips the believer "unto all good works."

When one considers all that is promised in these few verses, one wonders why Christians run after all kinds of other ideas that are in the world. God Himself says concerning His Word:

> So shall my word be that goeth forth out of my mouth: it shall not return unto me void, but it shall accomplish that which I please, and it shall prosper in the thing whereto I sent it (Isaiah 55:11).

God stands behind His Word and will cause it to do according to what He pleases. His Word will not fail.

Some people say they tried following the Bible but it didn't work for them. Could it be that they were at cross purposes with what God wanted to accomplish? The Word of God is to accomplish His will, and the only way it can accomplish an individual's will is if one desires God's will to be done. Even in the most extreme circumstances, the prayer, "Thy will be done," is the best because God's will is always best. Perhaps one reason people are interested in what the world says is because they want to fulfill their own purposes. Yet, even a babe in Christ, who is trusting in God's Word, will find that God is faithful to do what He has promised.

While we have already discussed the following Scripture, we cannot leave it out of this section because it reveals the supernatural work of God's Word:

> For the word of God is quick, and powerful, and sharper than any twoedged sword, piercing even to the dividing asunder of soul and spirit, and of the joints and marrow, and is a discerner of the thoughts and intents of the heart. Neither is there any creature that is not manifest in his sight: but all things are naked and opened unto the eyes of him with whom we have to do (Hebrews 4:12,13).

After reading and meditating on the breadth and length and depth and height of what this verse says, how can any Christian neglect reading the Bible or fail to trust what it says?

The Holy Spirit and the Word of God

The Holy Spirit indwells believers and enables them to know and understand Scripture. He also enables believers to obey the Word. Jesus promised His disciples that He would send the Holy Spirit to live in them and to reveal truth to them:

> And I will pray the Father, and he shall give you
> another Comforter, that he may abide with you for
> ever; Even the Spirit of truth; whom the world
> cannot receive, because it seeth him not, neither
> knoweth him: but ye know him; for he dwelleth
> with you, and shall be in you (John 14:16,17).

> But when the Comforter is come, whom I will send
> unto you from the Father, even the Spirit of truth,
> which proceedeth from the Father, he shall testify
> of me (John 15:26).

> Howbeit when he, the Spirit of truth, is come, he
> will guide you into all truth: for he shall not speak
> of himself; but whatsoever he shall hear, that
> shall he speak: and he will show you things to
> come (John 16:13).

Paul did not want to depend on his own human abilities or wisdom when he preached to the Corinthians. He depended upon the Holy Spirit to do the work in the hearts of the listeners as he spoke.

> And I, brethren, when I came to you, came not
> with excellency of speech or of wisdom, declaring
> unto you the testimony of God. For I determined
> not to know any thing among you, save Jesus
> Christ, and him crucified. And I was with you in
> weakness, and in fear, and in much trembling.
> And my speech and my preaching was not with
> enticing words of man's wisdom, but in demon-
> stration of the Spirit and of power: That your faith
> should not stand in the wisdom of men, but in the
> power of God (1 Corinthians 2:1-5).

The Holy Spirit is still at work when people read Scripture today. When the Word is received by faith and understood, it is by God's grace and power. When the Word is rejected, the Word is just as powerful and just as true, as Paul argues:

For what if some did not believe? shall their unbelief make the faith of God without effect? God forbid: yea, let God be true, but every man a liar; as it is written, That thou mightest be justified in thy sayings, and mightest overcome when thou art judged (Romans 3:3,4).

Apart from spiritual revelation by the Holy Spirit, human beings cannot truly know God's Word. While they may possess knowledge about doctrine, be able to understand from a limited human perspective, and even preach certain truths from Scripture, they cannot truly know the essence of God or the reality of what God says unless the Holy Spirit reveals such truth. The Holy Spirit helps believers to know, understand and obey Scripture. Paul explains:

> But as it is written, Eye hath not seen, nor ear heard, neither have entered into the heart of man, the things which God hath prepared for them that love him. But God hath revealed them unto us by his Spirit: for the Spirit searcheth all things, yea, the deep things of God. For what man knoweth the things of a man, save the spirit of man which is in him? even so the things of God knoweth no man, but the Spirit of God. Now we have received, not the spirit of the world, but the spirit which is of God; that we might know the things that are freely given to us of God. Which things also we speak, not in the words which man's wisdom teacheth, but which the Holy Ghost teacheth; comparing spiritual things with spiritual. But the natural man receiveth not the things of the Spirit of God: for they are foolishness unto him: neither can he know them, because they are spiritually discerned (1 Corinthians 2:9-14).

The Holy Spirit helps believers understand and know the Word of God and the riches of God's supply. The Holy Spirit teaches the believer through the Word, "comparing spiritual things with spiritual" (1 Corinthians 2:13). The Holy Spirit teaches the believer the Word of God and gives spiritual discernment. The Holy Spirit bears witness to the truth, "because the Spirit is truth" (1 John 5:6). So connected are the Word and the Spirit that Paul calls God's Word "the sword of the Spirit" (Ephesians 6:17).

The Holy Spirit not only enables believers to comprehend God's Word; the Holy Spirit enables believers to obey God's Word. Peter says:

> Seeing ye have purified your souls in obeying the truth through the Spirit unto unfeigned love of the brethren, see that ye love one another with a pure heart fervently: Being born again, not of corruptible seed, but of incorruptible, by the word of God, which liveth and abideth for ever (1 Peter 1:22,23).

Believers are not left to their own devices or to the psychological theories of men in order to know and obey truth. God has truly given believers all they need to know, understand, and obey His Word.

The Organization of Scripture

God in His wisdom did not write a volume of systematic theology. Nor did He simply write out a list of principles. God's Word is living and active. Just as every cell of the human body contains the entire chain of chromosomes, each section of Scripture contains God's life. Even before most of Scripture was yet written, David wrote the following about God's Law contained in His Word:

> The law of the LORD is perfect, converting the soul: the testimony of the LORD is sure, making wise the simple. The statutes of the LORD are right, rejoicing the heart: the commandment of the LORD is pure, enlightening the eyes. The fear of the LORD is clean, enduring for ever: the judgments of the LORD are true and righteous altogether. More to be

desired are they than gold, yea, than much fine gold: sweeter also than honey and the honeycomb. Moreover by them is thy servant warned: and in keeping of them there is great reward (Psalm 19:7-11).

During the time before much of the Old Testament had been written and before the entire New Testament had been written, David found much to live by in God's Word. Even today, with the canon of Scripture complete, believers find encouragement in these words of David.

Knowing the entire Bible is beneficial and to be desired, but one can gain a great deal from just a small portion. Many first-century believers may only have heard the Word of God or perhaps read portions of the Old Testament. They may also have heard or read one of Paul's letters. Nevertheless they were equipped with the whole counsel of God, which is compressed throughout Scripture. There are countless stories of believers who had only portions of Scripture, yet continued steadfast in their faith during persecution and when Bibles were forbidden. Radio programs beamed into then communist Russia dictated Scripture slowly so that people could write down sections of God's Word. How precious were those Scriptures to them and how effective, as they strengthened the believers during severe trials!

The Word of God is organized to point humans to God, to reveal His character, His power, His intelligence, His essence, His grace, His righteousness, His glory, His holiness, His justice, His mercy, and His love. Although God used many instruments of grace through which He breathed His Word, it is one unit from one source. It is revealed truth to be spiritually discerned and followed. God's presence pervades every jot and tittle so that even the smallest portion is of greater significance and power than all words spoken by man.

Nourishing the Soul with the Word of God.
Many believers experience various problems with

their emotions, thoughts, behavior, and personal relationships because they are spiritually malnourished. Rather than feasting on the Word of God and nourishing their souls, they feed on worldly fare. They try to live the Christian life on their own, rather than living in Christ and feeding on His Living Word.

Eating the Word of God is more than simply reading it. Feeding on the Word is reading with spiritual understanding, recognizing that the Author of the Word is the Lord God and that the Holy Spirit is present. It is carefully thinking about what is being read, cogitating, meditating, and desiring the Word to search one's soul as the "discerner of the thoughts and intents of the heart." The Word works together with the Spirit to convict the soul and change the heart (Hebrews 4:12,13).

Feeding on the Word is receiving instruction, wisdom, guidance, and strength. It is heeding the instruction, acting according to God's wisdom, following the guidance, and obeying by the power of God. Feeding on the Word leads to a deeper and fuller knowledge of Christ and therefore to a greater love for Him and a greater desire to obey Him. It changes the heart, increases faith, and enables believers to obey. God's Word is the true nourishment of the soul.

The offices of ministry that the Lord gave the church when He ascended into Heaven all speak forth the Word of God. Their calling is to minister God's Word for believers to grow more and more like Christ, for the work of the Lord to be accomplished, and for the Body of Christ to be built up. Speaking forth the Word through preaching, evangelizing, pastoring, and teaching gives counsel to each believer. If a pastor, for instance, feeds on and digests the Word as he studies a section of Scripture, the Holy Spirit will apply God's counsel to his life in particular. For him the application of the Word may be stronger faith, new insight into a situation in his life, encouragement, admonishment, greater love for the Lord, or conviction and repentance. As he recognizes how the Holy Spirit has applied the Scripture in his life, he can be confident that the same Holy Spirit will apply God's counsel to believers who hear his exposition of Scripture. The believers who hear his message may not receive the same specific application. The Word of God applies to every believer in the same general way, and the Holy Spirit applies God's counsel individually to each believer.

As a result of hearing a message that stressed Christ's obedience to the Father, two women had different responses. One of the points made during the sermon was that Jesus only did what His Father told Him to do. He did not obey the needs around Him. He only obeyed the Father. For instance, when the people demanded more bread, He did not give them what they asked for, but, instead, He told them that He was the true manna sent from heaven (John 6:57,58). When they sought miracles, He gave them truth. That sermon freed one woman from trying to fulfill too many needs. She needed to learn when to say, "No." The other woman's response to the same sermon was to become more involved in service. She needed to learn when to say, "Yes."

As believers learn the Word of God and the Holy Spirit applies God's counsel to their lives they, too, are equipped to minister. For instance, a Christian woman heard her pastor preach from a section of Scripture. As the Word was read and expounded, the Holy Spirit applied God's counsel to her. That very day she had an opportunity to obey the Word and thereby blessed her family. The next day she met another believer who was experiencing problems of living. As they conversed, the woman who received and obeyed God's counsel shared that same section of Scripture with her friend. The friend heard the Word and the Holy Spirit applied the counsel of God to her. Later, the second woman who received the Lord's counsel might have an opportunity to obey, and the effects would spread from person to person. Love and truth come from God and then flow throughout the Body of Christ.

The counsel of the Lord comes from His Word applied by the Holy Spirit. It is meant to be passed from one saint to another as nourishment flows through the body from cell to cell. Believers pass the counsel of the Lord to one another both by word and by deed. The Lord speaks directly through His Word and as believers study and obey the Bible they receive spiritual nourishment and are changed. Then, they have opportunities to minister that Word to fellow believers. When they do, the Word is living and active, and nourishment flows from one believer to another by the grace of God. As God's Word flows from one to another, each one receives that which is necessary for the edification of the Body of Christ to the glory of God.

Sufficient for Life and Godliness

God has truly given His children all that is necessary for living the Christian life—Jesus, the Holy Spirit, and His Word. Christians have a never-ending supply. Oh the depths and riches of God's Word! What a guide for living! What a perfect standard by which to evaluate one's own walk with the Lord! What a resource for daily living! What a rich supply of wisdom for helping and encouraging one another along the way! What a revelation whereby believers can come to know the Lord more and more completely!

Peter speaks about the sufficiency of God and His Word right at the beginning of his second epistle:

> Simon Peter, a servant and an apostle of Jesus Christ, to them that have obtained like precious faith with us through the righteousness of God and our Saviour Jesus Christ: Grace and peace be multiplied unto you through the knowledge of God, and of Jesus our Lord, According as his divine power hath given unto us all things that pertain unto life and godliness, through the knowledge of him that hath called us to glory and virtue: Whereby are given unto us exceeding great and

precious promises: that by these ye might be partakers of the divine nature, having escaped the corruption that is in the world through lust (2 Peter 1:1-4).

Notice how grace and peace are increased "through the knowledge of God, and of Jesus our Lord." God reveals Himself through His Word.

Next the passage says very directly that by His divine power He has given to believers "all things that pertain unto life and godliness, through the knowledge of him." God's supernatural power works to reveal Himself and His Word to believers, enabling them to live godly lives. God gives "exceeding great and precious promises" regarding both salvation and sanctification. Believers live by Christ's life in them as revealed in God's Word.

Since God supplies all that a believer requires to live a godly life, Peter continues with the believer's response to such marvelous provisions.

And beside this, giving all diligence, add to your faith virtue; and to virtue knowledge; and to knowledge temperance; and to temperance patience; and to patience godliness; and to godliness brotherly kindness; and to brotherly kindness charity (2 Peter 1:5-7).

The believer is not passive here, but active, "giving all diligence." Faith is not passive. Faith is busy acting on God's truth. From faith comes virtue, which is godly, moral living, which then leads to knowledge, self-control, patience, godliness (reflecting Christ), which leads to brotherly kindness and love. Then Peter declares that "if these things be in you, and abound, they make you that ye shall neither be barren nor unfruitful in the knowledge of our Lord Jesus Christ" (2 Peter 1:8).

If believers possess all these characteristics in addition to all that is necessary for life and godliness and the "exceeding great and precious promises," why does anyone look anywhere else? Peter answers that question in the very next verse. He says, "But he that lacketh these things is blind, and cannot see afar off, and hath forgotten that he was purged from his old sins" (2 Peter 1:9). He has reverted to the ways of the flesh, if he was ever converted in the first place. Those who say that the Bible is not enough or that it is not relevant to their needs fail to see the full provision for life in Christ.

Peter urges believers to "give diligence to make your calling and election sure: for if ye do these things, ye shall never fall" (2 Peter 1:10). God has given all that is necessary for life and godliness, and He supplies the ability to live godly lives. He has even given the faith, which enables believers to live victorious lives to His glory. These abundant provisions supplied by the righteousness and grace of God include all that is necessary for salvation and sanctification. Peter continues by saying, "For so an entrance shall be ministered unto you abundantly into the everlasting kingdom of our Lord and Saviour Jesus Christ" (2 Peter 1:11).

The importance of knowing and remembering God's righteousness, truth, promises, provisions, love, mercy and all He has revealed cannot be over-emphasized. Peter says, "Wherefore I will not be negligent to put you always in remembrance of these things, though ye know them, and be established in the present truth" (2 Peter 1:12). As believers, we need to keep on remembering what God has said. We need to remind one another and encourage one another to know what God has said that we might be "established in the present truth" and live according to the whole counsel of God by grace through faith.

7

Salvation and Sanctification in the Care of Souls

The care of souls involves both salvation and sancti-fication. The care of souls ministers to individuals in all matters of life and conduct with the goal that sinful souls become holy both in position and in practical liv-ing. The Lord of glory both saves and sanctifies. Lost souls are translated from the kingdom of darkness into the kingdom of light (Colossians 1:13).

The care of souls in the Body of Christ has contin-ued throughout the centuries from the inception of the church. However, whenever the wisdom of men has been added to the Word of God and the work of the Holy Spirit, the care of souls ministry has become distorted. When doctrines of salvation and sanctification are mod-ified according to external philosophies, metaphysics, "science falsely so-called," or any other system of

thought that seeks to understand man and prescribe
other means of salvation and change, the results
include legalism, fallacious faith, counterfeit conver-
sions, stunted spiritual growth and, worst of all, a
demeaning of Christ, the Holy Spirit, and the Word of
God.

The care of souls has been seriously compromised
through the Roman Catholic system of indulgences and
the faulty understanding and practices of confession
and penance. The Protestant Reformation sought to correct those errors. In seeking to base their faith entirely
on Scripture, the Reformers emphasized the doctrines
of justification by faith alone and the priesthood of all
believers. The doctrine of justification by faith alone set
believers free from misplaced trust in external acts for
their salvation. The scriptural doctrine of sanctification
brought a greater understanding of what it means to
walk according to the Spirit by faith within the context
of the mutual care of believers in the Body of Christ.

While pastors and elders fulfilled responsibilities to
care for souls through teaching and preaching, each
member of the Body of Christ was encouraged and
admonished to be a true disciple of Christ in both his
inner and outer life. He was to use Scripture "for doctrine, for reproof, for correction, for instruction in righteousness" just as Paul had written in his letter to
Timothy, "That the man of God may be perfect, thor-
oughly furnished unto all good works" (2 Timothy
3:16,17).

Believers were to study the Word not only for their
own growth, but also to encourage, admonish, exhort,
rebuke, console, forgive and love one another. They
were also to care for one another in the practical affairs
of life. The fellowship of the Spirit calls for the kind of
care that follows Paul's admonition:

> Let nothing be done through strife or vainglory;
> but in lowliness of mind let each esteem other bet-
> ter than themselves. Look not every man on his

own things, but every man also on the things of others (Philippians 2:3,4).

The Reformers returned to the Bible as their basis for preaching the Gospel and teaching doctrines of sanctified living. However, the means of sanctification were not to be a legalistic series of efforts separated from faith. Indeed, Martin Luther emphasized the Scriptural truth that "the just shall live by faith" (Romans 1:17; Galatians 3:11; Hebrews 10:38). Thus, the care of souls was back on the right track.

The only way for the care of souls to continue on the right track is for biblical doctrines of both salvation and sanctification to be known and clearly taught so that believers are not "tossed to and fro, and carried about with every wind of doctrine" (Ephesians 4:14). In looking at the progression of various errors and excesses in beliefs about how the Christian life is to be lived, one can see the rigidity of legalism, drifts into experiential mysticism, the sloppy agape of easy believism, and the intrusion of philosophies and psychologies of the world. Yet, all through the New Testament the Christian life is expressed through faith and obedience. The Epistles especially present a clear picture of what it is to be a Christian and how the Christian's faith is expressed both privately in the heart and publicly in one's demeanor.

God is the one who works in each believer all that is necessary for both salvation and sanctification. He does this through His Word, unaided by the wisdom of men or "science falsely so-called." He does not need man-made psychological systems to fill in the details for practical application. The Holy Spirit does that. He can complete in a person the application of the Word of God to his particular life and circumstances. For biblical principles to be set out as pills, or for men to assume to know the inner workings of another person's heart, or for any human to consider himself an expert of the soul is to ignore the nature of what it is to be human. Not all people are the same. Not all circumstances are equal. God does not work with everyone in exactly the same way. He allows circumstances, including difficulties and sorrows, that He will use for good in conforming His child into the image of His own dear Son (Romans 8:28,29). He gives His Word to reveal Himself, to search the heart, to enlighten the mind, to give knowledge, wisdom, discernment and direction, and to bring about those changes that will make His child more like Christ. The Holy Spirit works inside to enable the believer to know, understand, apply, and obey the Word of God.

Salvation

How essential it is to remember from whence each of us has come. Paul graphically describes every individual's depraved condition and God's great love, mercy, and justice whereby He gives new life:

> And you hath he quickened, who were dead in trespasses and sins: Wherein in time past ye walked according to the course of this world, according to the prince of the power of the air, the spirit that now worketh in the children of disobedience: Among whom also we all had our conversation in times past in the lusts of our flesh, fulfilling the desires of the flesh and of the mind; and were by nature the children of wrath, even as others. But God, who is rich in mercy, for his great love wherewith he loved us, Even when we were dead in sins, hath quickened us together with Christ, (by grace ye are saved;) And hath raised us up together, and made us sit together in heavenly places in Christ Jesus: That in the ages to come he might show the exceeding riches of his grace in his kindness toward us through Christ Jesus. For by grace are ye saved through faith; and that not of yourselves: it is the gift of God: Not of works, lest any man should boast. For we are his workman-

ship, created in Christ Jesus unto good works, which God hath before ordained that we should walk in them (Ephesians 2:1-10).

Every individual, except Jesus Christ, was born in sin and is "dead in trespasses and sins" until God, "who is rich in mercy, for his great love wherewith he loved us," gives new life. There is no way a person can save himself from his own sinful nature, but God has provided a way through the death and Resurrection of Christ. People are saved by God through faith. When they are saved they are given new life enabling them to choose God's way. When they receive God's love they respond in love through obedience.

While all of these spiritual transactions are made individually between God and each person, they are not isolated occurrences. They happen in the Body of Christ as each person serves according to the gifts, callings, and opportunities God gives. One may preach, another encourage, another excel in hospitality, another comfort, another give practical help, another exhort, another pray, another show mercy, but all can be used by God both to plant seeds of new life and harvest souls for the kingdom.

Sanctification

Once a person is converted by grace through faith, he begins a brand new life. While each believer is immediately a saint and is holy, in that he is set apart for God and sanctified by the Holy Spirit, he begins as a babe in Christ. As each believer grows, he is to become more like Christ. The fruit of the Spirit will become apparent in the believer's life. After all, those who have been saved by grace through faith "are his workmanship, created in Christ Jesus unto good works, which God hath before ordained that we should walk in them" (Ephesians 2:10). It is reasonable to expect external evidence of the internal work that Christ accomplishes in the lives of Christians. If there is no evidence of salvation and sanctification in what a person thinks, says and does, it may be that the person is not saved and needs yet to be converted and born again.

There are numerous opportunities for people to hear a watered-down gospel where people suppose that if they say a few words they have secured everlasting salvation without ever having been confronted with their own depravity and without ever having been truly converted. If such is the case, the person is trying to live the Christian life by means of the flesh. That is one reason why psychological counseling is so very popular in the professing church. If there is no new life, there is no spiritual growth. The true Gospel will not coddle the flesh or encourage people to feel like victims of circumstances. A clear presentation of the Gospel includes the conviction and eternal consequences of sin as well as the Good News that Christ died for sinners, rose from the grave and provided the only way of salvation by grace through faith.

One of the biggest errors in the care of souls is to assume that a person is truly converted when he is not. The person ministering the care of souls may need to confront this issue of salvation with the one who is seeking help in overcoming problems of living. While, on the one hand, only God knows the heart, on the other hand, there are certain biblical doctrines that can and should be used when talking with a person about his relationship with God through Jesus. Failure to do so can lead to a great waste of time. Moreover, it is a great injustice.

An external sign of one who is not saved is when one claims to be converted but continues on in sin. Here again, only God knows the heart. However, one who continues in known sin, especially after being mercifully confronted and patiently instructed, may not be saved. In such cases clear teachings about the Law (which reveals the destitute condition of the sinner) and the Gospel (the only salvation from sin and death) need to be given.

A Christian man was concerned about the spiritual condition of people who were regularly attending his church, but seemed to lack vibrancy in their Christianity. He decided to visit each family in the congregation to gently explore the reality of their faith. Although he fully expected to find most to be true believers who had, perhaps, lost their first love (Revelation 2:4), he found many who were trusting their own morality and good works to get them to heaven. They had identified with a "Christian" culture and morality, but they did not have an accurate understanding of salvation by grace through faith. They did not understand that people can do nothing to merit or maintain their own salvation. Nor did they truly discern that Christ's death and Resurrection are the basis for regeneration, salvation, justification, sanctification, and final glorification. Although they had listened to many sermons, they had failed to comprehend the nature of salvation. As this man simply and clearly presented the Gospel to them, some were given ears to hear, faith to believe, and new life in Christ.

When a person is truly saved by God through faith, he is given new life. Jesus Christ Himself purchased salvation through His death on the cross. He also provided the means of sanctification through His Resurrection from death unto His rightful position at the right hand of the Father. He, Himself, is the believer's life. Paul rejoiced in this fact when He declared:

> I am crucified with Christ: nevertheless I live; yet not I, but Christ liveth in me: and the life which I now live in the flesh I live by the faith of the Son of God, who loved me, and gave himself for me (Galatians 2:20).

The life of Christ in the believer stands in stark contrast to human beings trying to better themselves through man-made systems or even through biblical principles devoid of Christ's life.

Paul made this extremely clear when he upbraided the Galatians for adding various works and means to the salvation wrought by Christ. He wrote:

O foolish Galatians, who hath bewitched you, that ye should not obey the truth, before whose eyes Jesus Christ hath been evidently set forth, crucified among you? This only would I learn of you, Received ye the Spirit by the works of the law, or by the hearing of faith? Are ye so foolish? having begun in the Spirit, are ye now made perfect by the flesh?" (Galatians 3:1-3).

Indeed, even God's glorious, perfect Law could not save or sanctify them. If that had been possible, Christ's death would not have been necessary. Therefore, Paul argues that a person is to live the Christian life in the same way as he was saved in the first place—by grace through faith in the finished work of Christ and the ongoing work of Christ in the believer.

Paul urges believers to continue in sanctification as they began and warns them not to use other means for their Christian walk:

As ye have therefore received Christ Jesus the Lord, so walk ye in him: Rooted and built up in him, and stablished in the faith, as ye have been taught, abounding therein with thanksgiving. Beware lest any man spoil you through philosophy and vain deceit, after the tradition of men, after the rudiments of the world, and not after Christ. For in him dwelleth all the fulness of the Godhead bodily. And ye are complete in him, which is the head of all principality and power" (Colossians 2:6-10).

First Paul describes how to live the Christian life: "As ye have therefore received Christ Jesus the Lord, so walk ye in him: Rooted and built up in him, and stablished in the faith, as ye have been taught, abounding therein with thanksgiving." Just as believers received

Christ Jesus the Lord through faith, they are to continue their life in Him through faith. Next Paul tells them what to avoid and he gives the reason: because all one needs to live the Christian life is in Christ, "For in him dwelleth all the fulness of the Godhead bodily." If the fulness of the Godhead dwells in Christ and Christ is our life, is there any lack? What could "philosophy and vain deceit, after the tradition of men, after the rudiments of the world" add?

Unfortunately many quarters of the church have fallen for psychological philosophies and vain deceit in their attempts to help believers. Evangelical theologians have not only sorely neglected the practical side of sanctification; they have given it over to psychologized pastoral studies. Some have even devised psychological systems for sanctification. Even some, who have sought to help believers along the way through a biblical approach, have followed the psychological way to some degree. But, any approach that can be managed by the flesh fails, because it strengthens the flesh, rather than exposing its futility for spiritual growth. Any approach that feeds the flesh will fail to accomplish what the Bible tells believers to do with the flesh: to count it dead, to mortify its deeds, and to put it off (Romans 6:6-11; Romans 8:13; Ephesians 4:22; Colossians 3:9).

Every true believer is in the process of sanctification and growth until all are conformed to Christ. The goal is Christ and the means is Christ Himself, working in the believer through the Word of God and the the Holy Spirit. Since the goal is Christ and the means to that goal is also Christ, all believers need to be reminded and encouraged to pay more attention to Christ than themselves.

Many try to change their sinful behavior by focusing on themselves and then trying to change. They may even memorize verses that tell them to forgive their brother, to love their spouse, and to be slow to anger. But, the unforgiveness, the lack of love, and the anger continue. They are looking in the wrong direction, at themselves. Yet, if they turn their gaze to Christ and remember His great love for them and the cost He paid to secure their salvation, their love for Him may be renewed. If they remember that the Holy Spirit is in them to enable them to change, they will be encouraged in their faith and act accordingly.

As they consider the lengths to which Christ went to secure their pardon and as they have a passion to follow Christ, forgiveness for others will come. As they look on Christ's great love, they will be filled with love for others. They will remember that God loved them when they were still sinners and purchased their salvation when they had done nothing to deserve new life. Then, when that love flows through them they will love others, not by looking at themselves or trying harder, but by looking at Christ. And as they look at the patience God has with them, they will grow in patience and be less inclined to anger. All true Christian life flows from Christ in them. Beholding the Savior fixes their eyes to the goal of loving the Lord with their entire beings, loving their neighbors as they love themselves, and loving fellow believers as Christ loves them.

Impediments to Sanctification.

The first impediment to sanctification is a counterfeit conversion. Perhaps there has only been an intellectual assent or a brief response to an emotional appeal. Jesus' parable of the various soils reveals the fact that though some may seem to receive the Word with great enthusiasm, they have no continuing life in them (Matthew 13). There are lifeless professions of faith and false believers. That is why Paul says, "Examine yourselves, whether ye be in the faith; prove your own selves. Know ye not your own selves, how that Jesus Christ is in you, except ye be reprobates?" (2 Corinthians 13:5).

True salvation begins the ongoing process of sanctification. If there is true life in Christ, there will be growth and fruit. Christians don't simply turn to a new set of rules when they are born again. Instead, they receive new life that follows the standards of Scripture and reflects the very life of Christ in them. Scripture is the standard that describes the Christian life which follows salvation and the gift of new life.

Another impediment to sanctification is the influence of the world. In His prayer to His Father, as recorded in John 17, Jesus refers to His disciples as being "not of the world, even as I am not of the world" (John 17:14). The Apostle John teaches believers:

> Love not the world, neither the things that are in the world. If any man love the world, the love of the Father is not in him. For all that is in the world, the lust of the flesh, and the lust of the eyes, and the pride of life, is not of the Father, but is of the world. And the world passeth away, and the lust thereof: but he that doeth the will of God abideth for ever (1 John 2:15-17).

Many Christians who do not consider themselves lovers of the world nevertheless do love psychological teachings of the world, such as those developed by Freud, Jung, Adler, Maslow, Rogers, Ellis, and other secular theorists. While they may not embrace such systems in their totality, they pick and choose what to them sounds biblical. But a seeming echo of God's Word is not God's Word. Each psychological system is accompanied by a separate voice with many other things to say that have no basis in divine truth or even in science.

Even as we encourage believers to minister to one another the truth of God, we are gravely concerned about the psychological ideas that may have already been accepted and assumed not only to be true, but to be further understandings or applications of God's Word. Rather than one believer ministering the nourishment of the Word to another believer, we fear that some believers have already consumed so much psychology along the way that they will attempt to give a mixed meal—a warmed-over, left-over of psychoheresy pie.

The following is a brief example of how psychological ideas can set people in the wrong direction. A husband and wife (we'll call them Joe and Ellen) were experiencing serious problems in their marriage. Joe admitted he had a problem with lust. Ellen loved him and felt it was her duty to keep him away from places where he would be tempted. Joe did not want his wife to restrict his activities. Nevertheless, he did feel somewhat guilty and wanted to be relieved from his preoccupation with women's bodies. Because he was a professing Christian, he looked for answers in the church. However, he wanted relief without dying to self and without really having to do anything to overcome his sinful habit of lusting after women.

He complained about his problem to another professing Christian, who diagnosed his problem as low self-esteem. The solution was to love himself more and raise his self-esteem. He immediately bought into the idea. Like magic his guilty feelings disappeared and he was free to continue indulging in lust until the day when his self-esteem would be high enough to change. To accomplish his goal Joe started seeing a "Christian psychologist" and joined a 12-step group. His journey took him further away from the Lord, the church, and his family.

While this may seem like an extreme example, it is more common than one might imagine. It also reveals the direction psychological notions espoused by Christians can take a person. That is why we continue to endeavor to expose psychological teachings along the way. They creep in so subtly that one must be on guard to discern truth by assiduously studying Scripture. Paul exhorted Timothy: "Study to show thyself approved unto God, a workman that needeth not to be ashamed, rightly dividing the word of truth" (2 Timothy 2:15). How much we need this kind of teaching. If Joe had been studying Scripture, he should have known better than to follow such advice. Moreover, if he had kept his eyes on Christ in the first place, he would not have been so eager to look lustfully at women.

Unfortunately, many of these psychological ideas, such as self-esteem, are woven into sermons. They are common fare in many churches. Even in churches where the preaching on Sunday mornings is solidly biblical, members may still follow the psychological way throughout the week. That is because of the many voices coming into the church in books and other materials and coming into homes through various media. Although such members listen to the sermons, they also feed on psychological notions and run their lives according to the wisdom of men rather than the pure Word of God. Their lives during the week fail to line up with such biblical standards as obedience to Christ (John 14:15), the fruit of the Spirit (Galatians 5:22,23), good deeds (Ephesians 2:10), and godly service (John 12:26). When they face problems of living, they have little experience in living according to the Word of God and the life of Christ in them.

It appears that such people have not fed on God's Word or they only follow it superficially. Why do we say that? Because of the secular manner in which professing Christians respond to problems of living, both in their own lives and in the lives of others. Many refer to psychology in hallowed voices. They admonish fellow believers to feel good about themselves and increase their self esteem. If a fellow believer has serious problems, they strongly recommend counseling, and by this they generally mean counseling done by someone trained in psychology. We have heard Bible scholars speak of the Freudian unconscious as if it is factual, even though Freud's theories are now discredited. Instead, we all need to think with the mind of Christ, according to the truth revealed in the Word of God and not according to the myths of men.

Abiding in Christ

When a person is given new life, he is converted from a sinner to a saint by justification through faith (John 1:12-13; Romans 5:1; 1 Corinthians 1:2). Each person who is saved by grace through faith is indwelt by Christ and is in Christ. Jesus accomplishes the primary work of placing us in Himself through His death and Resurrection. He also comes to live in believers to enable them to abide in Him and live according to His Word.

Abiding in Jesus is living in the midst of His love. This means believing His love and His Word even when every circumstance and feeling may deny that very love. The Apostle Paul understood the importance of this love relationship, and he prayed for believers:

> That he [God] would grant you, according to the riches of his glory, to be strengthened with might by his Spirit in the inner man; That Christ may dwell in your hearts by faith; that ye, being rooted and grounded in love, May be able to comprehend with all saints what is the breadth, and length, and depth, and height; And to know the love of Christ, which passeth knowledge, that ye might be filled with all the fulness of God (Ephesians 3:16-19).

Abiding in Christ is living in a love relationship with Him in which we receive and believe His love and by which we express our love for Him through obedience (John 14:15, 21). Since all knowledge, understanding, and wisdom are in Him, and, since He loves us beyond what we can even comprehend, to obey Him is not a legalistic act, but one of faith and love.

One might think abiding in Christ has more to do with "sensing His presence" than attending or giving heed to His presence. However, attending to Christ's presence has to do with paying attention to reality, the very fact that Christ is present in the believer and that He has promised never to leave or forsake His own.

Sensing His presence, on the other hand, has to do with feelings, which come and go.

For instance, let us suppose that a person has just enjoyed a time of prayer and quiet meditation on the Word of God and has sensed God's presence in those quiet moments. Minutes later, however, that same person is in the midst of people making demands and circumstances going awry. He becomes frustrated and angry, not only because of the immediate situation, but because he feels he has lost the presence of God. Yet, God is there. Christ has not left him. But, rather than turning to Christ in the midst of the struggle, he feels defeated and lost. Later, as he turns his thoughts back to the Lord, he sees his error. He may then understand that remaining in Christ's presence is acknowledging Him, believing He is there, and acting accordingly.

God's Word gives what we need to know about living the Christian life. In His Word we will find doctrine, instruction, guidance, and all the information necessary for living the Christian life. However, because we all receive so much unbiblical input from living in the world, we need to be reminded again and again about the source for godly living. That source is Jesus Christ Himself, "in whom are hid all the treasures of wisdom and knowledge" (Colossians 2:3). Much of the care of souls involves reminding one another of what it is to be a Christian and how the Lord has designed sanctification to occur. Just after his brief description of sanctification in his second letter, the Apostle Peter says:

> Wherefore the rather, brethren, give diligence to make your calling and election sure: for if ye do these things, ye shall never fall: For so an entrance shall be ministered unto you abundantly into the everlasting kingdom of our Lord and Saviour Jesus Christ. Wherefore I will not be negligent to put you always in remembrance of these things, though ye know them, and be established in the present truth. Yea, I think it meet, as

long as I am in this tabernacle, to stir you up by putting you in remembrance (2 Peter 1:10-13).

The reminders are both to keep fellow believers on the right path and to motivate them to continue to walk by faith in obedience to Christ.

8

Living and Ministering by Faith

All believers are competent to minister to one another in the Body of Christ by grace through faith in God and in His Word. They are saved by grace through faith, they are sanctified by grace through faith, and they are to live and minister to one another by grace through faith. After they believe God for salvation through the death and Resurrection of Christ, they are to continue their walk in the Spirit through the life of the resurrected Christ living in them. As they live by faith they are competent to minister God's grace to one another, believing that God is sovereign and true to His Word—that He has given them "all things that pertain unto life and godliness" (2 Peter 1:3). If, however, their faith is undermined or misplaced, their confidence in God and their competence to minister diminish. Therefore we want to encourage believers to live according to all that God has promised—His "exceeding great and precious promises: that by these ye might be partakers of the divine nature, having escaped the corruption that is in the world through lust" (2 Peter 1:4).

What Kind of Faith?

The Bible declares that "the just shall live by faith" (Romans 1:17; Galatians 3:11; Hebrews 10:38). Those who are counted righteous by grace through faith have new life, and they are to continue living by faith. But what kind of faith is that? There are those who have reduced faith to a name-it-and-claim it sort of manipulation to get what they want from God. There are also many non-Christians who believe in the importance of faith. No one is without some kind of faith, even if it is just the expectation that a chair that has been sturdy in the past is still safe to sit on.

The Bible describes faith as "the substance of things hoped for, the evidence of things not seen" (Hebrews 11:1). Faith is expectation without external confirmation. It is belief or confidence that a future expectation will come to pass even though there is no visible proof on which to base the anticipation. The belief may be based on past events, such as the chair example. The belief may be in a person who has previously fulfilled expectations, such as a baby's faith in its mother for food. Or, faith may be based on promises made by those who for some reason are trusted.

People place faith in themselves, in other people, and in ideologies, methods, technologies, and physical objects. Everyone, from the most gullible to the most skeptical, exercises some kind of faith. It is a natural ingredient in effective human relations. A measure of trust is necessary for business to be conducted and to manage other affairs. In fact, doctors, dentists, lawyers, and other professionals display their degrees and other credentials to engender faith. Psychotherapists and some biblical counselors do the same.

In psychotherapy, faith ultimately rests in the therapist to bring forth solutions to problems and healing for the emotions. One researcher in the field of psychotherapy finds that "the essential ingredient of this relationship is that the patient has confidence in the therapist's competence and in his desire to be of help."[1]

Many Christians not only have faith in psychological counselors; they have faith in the process of counseling and in the underlying theories, systems, techniques, and training. In fact, Dr. Thomas Szasz declares: "Ritualized psychiatric interventions, I maintain, have no real therapeutic power, beyond that which the patient imputes to them."[2]

Placebo (a fake pill or fake treatment) is dependent on a patient's faith in the pill or treatment, which he believes to be real. Dr. Arthur Shapiro, a clinical professor of psychiatry, suggests that apparent positive effects of psychotherapy may actually be the placebo effect. He says, "Just as bloodletting was perhaps the massive placebo technique of the past, so psychoanalysis—and its dozens of psychotherapy offshoots—is the most used placebo of our time."[3]

Indeed all psychological counseling and much of what is currently called "biblical counseling" rest on faith in the therapist or counselor and faith in the counseling process, system, theories, techniques, training and other trappings. When one considers that there are over 450 different systems of psychological therapy and that they all seem to work equally well, one must conclude that something other than the specific system of therapy is at work. Could it be faith? Researcher Dr. Jerome Frank says:

> The apparent success of healing methods based on all sorts of ideologies and methods compels the conclusion that the healing power of faith resides in the patient's state of mind, not in the validity of its object.[4]

If faith has that much power in itself, regardless of the object of that faith, Christians should exercise their faith wisely. Faith that is merely a person's state of mind was the kind of faith that Eve exercised when she trusted what the serpent said in the Garden. Instead of continuing to trust God, Eve shifted her trust to the serpent as he made false promises. Yes, her faith was powerful enough to affect the entire human race through Adam, but that is not the kind of faith God honors. The Israelites grossly sinned against God whenever they trusted in idols, soothsayers, or the arm of the flesh instead of God. Numerous systems of men have been established that draw faith and trust away from God.

Saving Faith

Faith is essential for Christians, but not just any kind of faith. Their faith is to be in God and in His Word. Their entire Christian life begins by grace through faith and continues by grace through faith. The glorious truth of justification by faith freed the Reformers from bondage to an erroneous theology of works. Many who profess Christ do trust God for their justification. They look forward to eternal life based upon the promise of the Gospel, clearly stated in numerous places in Scripture. They believe that God sent His Son to be a sacrifice for their sins and that they are "justified freely by his grace through the redemption that is in Christ Jesus" (Romans 3:24) and that they are "justified by faith without the deeds of the law" (Romans 3:28).

> For by grace are ye saved through faith; and that not of yourselves: it is the gift of God: Not of works, lest any man should boast For we are his workmanship, created in Christ Jesus unto good works, which God hath before ordained that we should walk in them (Ephesians 2:8-10).

Faith is essential to spiritual life. It is the first response of the believer in his walk with Christ and it is to continue throughout the Christian walk. Peter says that believers are "kept by the power of God through faith unto salvation ready to be revealed in the last time" (1 Peter 1:5). The walk of faith continues even through difficult circumstances:

> That the trial of your faith, being much more precious than of gold that perisheth, though it be tried with fire, might be found unto praise and honour and glory at the appearing of Jesus Christ: Whom having not seen, ye love; in whom, though now ye see him not, yet believing, ye rejoice with joy unspeakable and full of glory: Receiving the end of your faith, even the salvation of your souls 1 Peter 1:7-9).

While many Christians do continue to trust God for their final destination in glory, they often fail to trust Him for problems of living and turn to various outside counselors for help. Yet, if the Body of Christ is growing together in faith and ministering grace to one another in times of difficulty, they will deepen in their knowledge of God and continue to grow in faith.

Sanctifying Faith

Sanctifying faith is living by Christ's life. True Christian faith is more than a positive mind-set. The source of the Christian's faith is Christ Himself. The believer so identifies with Christ's death and Resurrection that he lives by Christ's faith. Paul puts it this way:

> I am crucified with Christ: nevertheless I live; yet not I, but Christ liveth in me: and the life which I now live in the flesh I live by the faith of the Son of God, who loved me, and gave himself for me (Galatians 2:20).

This describes the normal Christian life. It is not only for seasoned believers; it is true of every believer who is walking according to new life in Christ. When believers veer away from the truth of this verse they are living as pagans rather than as true Christians.

After believers receive new life by faith they are to live that life by faith in Christ, not by another system:

> As ye have therefore received Christ Jesus the Lord, so walk ye in him: Rooted and built up in him, and stablished in the faith, as ye have been taught, abounding therein with thanksgiving. Beware lest any man spoil you through philosophy and vain deceit, after the tradition of men, after the rudiments of the world, and not after Christ. For in him dwelleth all the fulness of the Godhead bodily. And ye are complete in him, which is the head of all principality and power (Colossians 2:6-10).

As they walk in Christ, according to His life by faith, their roots go deep into His life and they are built up and established in the faith. Paul warns believers not to be sidetracked with any other systems, not only because they have all they need in Christ, but also because these other systems will deprive them of experiencing the fulness of what they have in Christ. Their own life and their effectiveness in the Body of Christ will become diminished if they begin to trust the wisdom of men instead of Christ, who, being "the head of all principality and power," far exceeds any philosophies, psychologies, or other traditions of man.

Self-Examination

It is important to note that in this present era of psychological analysis and introspection, the only self-examination called for in Scripture is to determine whether one is "in the faith" and walking by faith: "Examine yourselves, whether ye be in the faith; prove your own selves. Know ye not your own selves, how that

Jesus Christ is in you, except ye be reprobates?" (2 Corinthians 13:5). Paul also warns believers that before they take Holy Communion they should examine themselves to see what sin they might be harboring so that they might confess, be cleansed, and renew their walk of faith, remembering that forgiveness comes through Christ's substitutionary death (1 Corinthians 11:28-31).

Self-examination is not the same as self-analysis. Rather than seeking insight into the self, Christians are to evaluate their inner and outer life according to biblical standards. The Bible is the standard for doctrine, for reproof when someone is not living according to the doctrines of Scripture, for correction, and for instruction in living according to righteousness by the power of God (2 Timothy 3:16,17). One looks at one's life in reference to God's Word, not in reference to psychological systems devised by humans.

With the Bible in hand, professing Christians can examine themselves to see if they believe God's Word, doubt it, or simply ignore it. Those who fail to believe that Christ's commandments proceed from His love will walk in the limitation of their own wisdom and the deception of their own ideas and imaginations. Those who fail to believe God's wisdom and disbelieve that sin has consequences live in the shadow of deception. Those who doubt God's Word and therefore His character are extremely vulnerable to temptation and sin. Or, they may say they believe the Bible, but have no external evidence of faith.

Here are some questions, that may be asked regarding faith: Do I really believe I am a sinner? Do I really believe that "all our righteousnesses are as filthy rags" (Isaiah 64:6) in the sight of God? Do I really believe that "all have sinned, and come short of the glory of God" (Romans 3:23)? Did Jesus pay my debt of sin by dying on the cross in my place? Is His blood sufficient to cover all my sin? Is He now living in me? Will He ever leave me or forsake me? Can I trust all His promises to me?

Living by Faith

Such questions may seem rather elementary, but they are necessary to examine oneself to see if one is indeed in the faith and walking by faith. There are professing Christians who fail to believe basic Bible doctrines, or, if they can mentally assent to them, they fail to live accordingly. Faith in God's Word and living by that faith are tested in those people who are experiencing problems of living, because such challenges tend to reveal the condition of one's faith. One may be weak and need encouragement and instruction. Another may recognize no resources in the self and simply trust God out of desperation. Another may forget God or avoid Him in the midst of problems. Another may look at troubles as opportunities to know God better.

Scripture describes what happens in believers by grace through faith as they trust God in the midst of difficulties:

> Therefore being justified by faith, we have peace with God through our Lord Jesus Christ: By whom also we have access by faith into this grace wherein we stand, and rejoice in hope of the glory of God. And not only so, but we glory in tribulations also: knowing that tribulation worketh patience; And patience, experience; and experience, hope: And hope maketh not ashamed; because the love of God is shed abroad in our hearts by the Holy Ghost which is given unto us (Romans 5:1-5).

Oh the riches available to believers who trust their Lord Jesus Christ, who has given them access by faith into God's grace! Not only are believers justified by faith with the hope of glory in eternity; believers can even "glory in tribulations," because they know that God will perfect them through difficulties. Not only does God bring them through, but He works His character and love in them through the Holy Spirit.

People often cringe at the thought of God using pain and difficult trials for spiritual growth. In fact, when those who are going through trials do "glory in tribulations," others refuse to think that God could be so cruel as to allow His children to suffer. But, that is exactly what Paul meant in Romans 5:1-5. **God uses the most difficult times in our lives and sometimes the most grueling pain to teach us, purify us, and use us for His glory.** An example of this is a dear saint by the name of Karin, who endured much physical pain over many years and is now with her Savior.

When Karin suffered kidney failure as a young woman, some well-meaning Christians prayed over her and told her that if she had enough faith she would be healed. Her faith grew, but she was not healed. Her father donated a kidney, but after four agonizing years of her body not accommodating his gracious gift, she had to have it removed. From then on she relied on dialysis and continued to deteriorate physically. Yet, the more pain she endured, the closer she drew to the Lord. The more she cried out to Him, the better she knew His presence, compassion, and sufficiency. She firmly believed that God was allowing these circumstances for His glory and she wanted to be a witness to family members and friends who did not know Him.

Karin relied on the sufficiency of Christ and the Word of God. When her body refused to accept her father's kidney, doctors who believed in a Freudian unconscious urged her into psychoanalysis, with the idea that she rejected her father in her unconscious. However, she had already tried various psychotherapies before she was converted to Christianity. She had found psychotherapy unhelpful and even harmful in the past. She no longer trusted the teachings of psychoanalysis or humanistic psychology. She now trusted the Lord.

At various times of increased pain and increasing physical problems, such as deteriorating vertebrae, friends who loved her urged her to see psychologically trained counselors to help her through the struggles.

Each time she explained that psychological systems had nothing for her. She assured her friends that Christ is sufficient. She trusted Christ only and did not want to add psychological counseling to help her meet the difficult challenges of her condition.

Even though her physical strength was diminished, Karin was deeply involved in the mutual care of souls. She asked for prayer and prayed for others. She graciously received help during her many hospitalizations, and when she had strength she reached out to help others. Besides helping at church, she would send notes of encouragement and share insights from God's Word as she met with other believers or visited on the phone. She faithfully testified to Christ's faithfulness.

Most people would not want to be shaped in the crucible of pain in which Karin was shaped. Yet, the Master's marvelous creativity conforming her to the image of Christ could be seen even while she walked among us. Her own faithfulness and love for the Lord inspired others to love and trust Jesus. As the love of the Holy Spirit flowed out of her life, we saw an example of Romans 5:1-5 over and over again.

James also writes about responding to trouble with confidence in God that, as one's faith is stretched, one grows in patience and wholeness.

> My brethren, count it all joy when ye fall into divers temptations; knowing this, that the trying of your faith worketh patience. But let patience have her perfect work, that ye may be perfect and entire, wanting nothing (James 1:2-4).

James also instructs believers to ask God for wisdom in the midst of problems. However, they are to ask in faith without wavering, but trusting God to show the way. In fact, if they consistently waver in faith, James calls them double minded and unstable.

> If any of you lack wisdom, let him ask of God, that giveth to all men liberally, and upbraideth not;

and it shall be given him. But let him ask in faith, nothing wavering. For he that wavereth is like a wave of the sea driven with the wind and tossed. For let not that man think that he shall receive any thing of the Lord. A double minded man is unstable in all his ways (James 1:5-8).

Faith is not an option for Christians:

But without faith it is impossible to please him: for he that cometh to God must believe that he is, and that he is a rewarder of them that diligently seek him (Hebrews 11:6).

But, how many people trust God only to a point and then turn to another system of help—another religion? All psychotherapies are religious in nature. They constitute religion rather than science. As believers trust the ways of men over the ways of God, they move further and further away from His help. Their faith is stunted and their usefulness in the Body of Christ is reduced. If they have placed faith in other systems of help, they will lead others astray into those systems.

While this book is meant to be an encouragement for believers to minister to one another in the Body of Christ, we are concerned that those who are not walking by faith may minister the ways of the world rather than the ways of God. We need to admonish each other not to trust the wisdom of men, but to rely on the Word of God, as Paul admonished the Corinthians: "That your faith should not stand in the wisdom of men, but in the power of God" (1 Corinthians 2:5). We need to encourage one another to "walk by faith, not by sight" (2 Corinthians 5:7).

Ministering by Grace through Faith

All true ministry in the Body of Christ is by faith. When Jesus was asked, "What shall we do, that we might work the works of God?" He replied, "This is the work of God, that ye believe on him whom he hath sent"

(John 6:28,29). Faith in Christ is the primary work and all other good works follow as a result of faith.

Believers need to be reminded and encouraged that it is actually possible to live by faith from moment to moment and day by day. Faith is not simply a mind-set to be donned during a worship service or during a set time of devotions. If a person only breathed air for a few hours during the week, he would not survive until the end of that week. Yet, many people who profess faith in Christ hardly even think of him during the week, let alone trust Him in every circumstance. That is why believers need to remind and encourage one another to believe God in practical matters. Often a babe in Christ, who has just newly trusted Christ and who "innocently" expects the rest of the Christians to be trusting Him as well, may be used mightily to remind older believers about their riches in Christ.

One fairly new believer, who had trusted in the wisdom of the world before being converted to Christ, learned and believed 1 Corinthians 10:13:

> There hath no temptation taken you but such as is common to man: but God is faithful, who will not suffer you to be tempted above that ye are able; but will with the temptation also make a way to escape, that ye may be able to bear it.

When other Christian women shared their problems with her, she was excited to tell them about her new "discovery" and would confidently quote the verse, explain the meaning of it, and apply it to their circumstances. She did not doubt the validity of God's promise and her faith encouraged others to trust Him, too, even though she was a fairly new believer.

Even more astounding than simply sharing 1 Corinthians 10:13 with others is when a new believer lives according to that verse in the sight of a local body of believers. Living the verse is an even greater testimony than talking about it, though both can be done by all Christians because of Christ and for the sake of building up His Body. This is simply one example of how faith can operate in a believer's life and minister grace to the rest of the Body. The advantage of a seasoned believer is that he has had the opportunity to live that verse over and over again. But, God may use even a babe in Christ to remind him again where he has previously found strength.

There are so many ways in which believers can and do minister to one another in the Body of Christ. As Christians believe God and love one another they discover all kinds of ways to express God's love and kindness to one another. Because of the creative power of God, believers often find creative ways to express God's love and care. As they trust God and His Word and as they trust him to enable them to minister to one another, they find God faithful. "As we have therefore opportunity, let us do good unto all men, especially unto them who are of the household of faith" (Galatians 6:10).

Faith is active in ministry and it is intrinsically joined with hope and love. Paul writes to the Thessalonians about:

> Remembering without ceasing your work of faith, and labour of love, and patience of hope in our Lord Jesus Christ, in the sight of God and our Father" (1 Thessalonians 1:3).

The work of faith is combined with labor of love and patience of hope. As believers walk by faith, their ministry will be in love and bring forth fruit. Just as the fruit of the Spirit comprises different qualities of the one fruit of the Spirit, so also faith, hope and love work together. God speaks in His Word and we respond in faith and hope, because we know we can trust Him who loves us and holds the universe in His hands. Faith, hope and love come from the life of Christ in the believer. By these, believers are to minister to one another to edify the Body of Christ.

Faith in Action

Faith is not a passive attitude. It is steadfast trust. And, it is acted on. Some may say one thing, but do another. That is not true faith. True faith in God brings consistency between belief on the inside and action on the outside. Believing, speaking, and acting line up. While James taught that we are saved by faith, he was concerned about those whose so-called faith was devoid of visible results. He wrote:

> What doth it profit, my brethren, though a man say he hath faith, and have not works? can faith save him? If a brother or sister be naked, and destitute of daily food, And one of you say unto them, Depart in peace, be ye warmed and filled; notwithstanding ye give them not those things which are needful to the body; what doth it profit? Even so faith, if it hath not works, is dead, being alone. Yea, a man may say, Thou hast faith, and I have works: show me thy faith without thy works, and I will show thee my faith by my works. Thou believest that there is one God; thou doest well: the devils also believe, and tremble. But wilt thou know, O vain man, that faith without works is dead? (James 2:14-20).

Indeed mutual care in the Body of Christ calls for more than mental assent to what the Bible says. Mutual care calls for faith that is expressed in words and action. Mutual care comes from such active faith that people are fed and clothed. Faith is extremely practical and, though it has a heavenly source, faith is exercised in very down-to-earth ways. Faith leads to service.

Action motivating faith can be seen in Hebrews 11, that great chapter on faith. Here we see faith in action. "By faith Abel offered unto God a more excellent sacrifice than Cain." "By faith Enoch. . . . By faith Noah. . . . By faith Abraham . . . . By faith Moses. . . . By faith Rahab. . . ." "By faith" each of these and others listed in Hebrews 11 did something in obedience to God. Faith was not simply mental assent. It was so active that many were tortured for their faith.

Our actions reveal our faith. For example, Paul says, "But if any provide not for his own, and specially for those of his own house, he hath denied the faith, and is worse than an infidel" (1 Timothy 5:8). On the other hand, faith is evidenced by actions of love and faithfulness in the midst of persecution:

> We are bound to thank God always for you, brethren, as it is meet, because that your faith groweth exceedingly, and the charity of every one of you all toward each other aboundeth; So that we ourselves glory in you in the churches of God for your patience and faith in all your persecutions and tribulations that ye endure (2 Thessalonians 1:3,4).

Even as he sees these believers walking in faith and ministering love to one another, Paul prays that they will continue to do so. He says:

> Wherefore also we pray always for you, that our God would count you worthy of this calling, and fulfil all the good pleasure of his goodness, and the work of faith with power: That the name of our Lord Jesus Christ may be glorified in you, and ye in him, according to the grace of our God and the Lord Jesus Christ (2 Thessalonians 1:11,12).

Faith is also a believer's weapon of defense, "the shield of faith, wherewith ye shall be able to quench all the fiery darts of the wicked" (Ephesians 6:16). Faith is joined with love to serve as a believer's armor, "the breastplate of faith and love" (1 Thessalonians 5:8). In his first letter to Timothy, Paul urges him to: "Fight the good fight of faith, lay hold on eternal life, whereunto thou art also called, and hast professed a good profession before many witnesses" (1 Timothy 6:12). In his second letter to Timothy, Paul says:

But watch thou in all things, endure afflictions, do the work of an evangelist, make full proof of thy ministry. For I am now ready to be offered, and the time of my departure is at hand. I have fought a good fight, I have finished my course, I have kept the faith: Henceforth there is laid up for me a crown of righteousness, which the Lord, the righteous judge, shall give me at that day: and not to me only, but unto all them also that love his appearing (2 Timothy 4:5-8).

Prayer

Paul lived by faith and prayed diligently for all believers, which is one of the most powerful ministries in the Body of Christ, not because of the person praying but because of the power and purposes of God. One of the simplest, yet most profound and effective ways all believers can minister is praying for one another. The following are wonderful examples of praying for one another:

And this I pray, that your love may abound yet more and more in knowledge and in all judgment; That ye may approve things that are excellent; that ye may be sincere and without offence till the day of Christ; Being filled with the fruits of righteousness, which are by Jesus Christ, unto the glory and praise of God (Philippians 1:9-11).

For this cause we also, since the day we heard it, do not cease to pray for you, and to desire that ye might be filled with the knowledge of his will in all wisdom and spiritual understanding; That ye might walk worthy of the Lord unto all pleasing, being fruitful in every good work, and increasing in the knowledge of God; Strengthened with all might, according to his glorious power, unto all patience and longsuffering with joyfulness; Giving thanks unto the Father, which hath made us meet to be partakers of the inheritance of the saints in light (Colossians 1:9-12).

For this cause I bow my knees unto the Father of our Lord Jesus Christ, Of whom the whole family in heaven and earth is named, That he would grant you, according to the riches of his glory, to be strengthened with might by his Spirit in the inner man; That Christ may dwell in your hearts by faith; that ye, being rooted and grounded in love, May be able to comprehend with all saints what is the breadth, and length, and depth, and height; And to know the love of Christ, which passeth knowledge, that ye might be filled with all the fulness of God (Ephesians 3:14-19).

Christ prayed for His disciples and taught them to pray. The evening before His crucifixion Jesus said to His disciples:

And whatsoever ye shall ask in my name, that will I do, that the Father may be glorified in the Son. If ye shall ask any thing in my name, I will do it John 14:13,14).

Praying "in Jesus' name" is not just tacking those words at the end of a prayer, but rather praying according to His character and according to His will. Selfish prayers have no guarantee of being answered, as James says: "Ye ask, and receive not, because ye ask amiss, that ye may consume it upon your lusts" (James 4:3). On the other hand, praying to the Father in Jesus' name, according to His very being, joins believers together with God's purposes for His glory.

Prayer is a great privilege given to believers. Moreover, they have confidence before God's throne because Christ is the "one mediator between God and men" (1 Timothy 2:5). Paul says: "I will therefore that men pray every where, lifting up holy hands, without wrath and doubting" (1 Timothy 2:8). The book of Hebrews continues this same theme of Christ as mediator:

Seeing then that we have a great high priest, that is passed into the heavens, Jesus the Son of God, let us hold fast our profession. For we have not an high priest which cannot be touched with the feeling of our infirmities; but was in all points tempted like as we are, yet without sin. Let us therefore come boldly unto the throne of grace, that we may obtain mercy, and find grace to help in time of need (Hebrews 4:14-16).

Faith and righteousness and prayer go together, for when believers exercise faith in God they live by Christ's righteousness and they pray for one another. James writes:

Is any among you afflicted? let him pray. Is any merry? let him sing psalms. Is any sick among you? let him call for the elders of the church; and let them pray over him, anointing him with oil in the name of the Lord: And the prayer of faith shall save the sick, and the Lord shall raise him up; and if he have committed sins, they shall be forgiven him. Confess your faults one to another, and pray one for another, that ye may be healed. The effectual fervent prayer of a righteous man availeth much (James 5:13-16).

Believers strengthen their faith as they pray. As they exercise their faith they come to know Christ better (2 Peter 1), and as they deepen in their knowledge of Christ, their faith grows. The Bible also teaches that "faith cometh by hearing, and hearing by the word of God" (Romans 10:17). The Word of God itself engenders faith. God uses the Word being preached to save sinners and He continues to use His Word to build faith.

As you grow in faith by hearing and obeying the Word, you are becoming ever more competent to minister the care of souls in the Body of Christ to the glory of God.

9

Ministering Hope to One Another

All believers are competent to minister to one another in the Body of Christ because their hope is in Christ. Hope empowers ministry with courage and confidence and allows the fruit of the Spirit to flourish. Hope fixes the eyes on Christ, not only for today, but also for the future. Hope motivates the believer to press on in devotion and service and to know Christ at each moment on the way to glory. Paul describes his hope in Christ as all-encompassing:

> Yea doubtless, and I count all things but loss for the excellency of the knowledge of Christ Jesus my Lord: for whom I have suffered the loss of all things, and do count them but dung, that I may win Christ, And be found in him, not having mine

own righteousness, which is of the law, but that which is through the faith of Christ, the righteousness which is of God by faith: That I may know him, and the power of his resurrection, and the fellowship of his sufferings, being made conformable unto his death; If by any means I might attain unto the resurrection of the dead. Not as though I had already attained, either were already perfect: but I follow after, if that I may apprehend that for which also I am apprehended of Christ Jesus. Brethren, I count not myself to have apprehended: but this one thing I do, forgetting those things which are behind, and reaching forth unto those things which are before, I press toward the mark for the prize of the high calling of God in Christ Jesus (Philippians 3:8-14).

Paul reveals the motivating power of hope. Suffering the loss of all things means nothing compared to knowing Christ and having the hope of going all the way with Christ into glory. While the image Paul presents is one of aiming for a goal, that goal is the hope of the Gospel. Paul does not want to miss one iota of what God has for him on the way. Yet he fixes his eye on the goal and presses on toward the "mark for the prize of the high calling of God in Christ Jesus." That high calling is in Christ and begins at new birth, reaches a culmination in glory and then continues throughout eternity. Such hope should motivate every believer to serve Christ with all his being.

Though Paul refers to himself pressing toward the mark, the powerful impact of this hope in Christ is not limited to the Apostles or even to a select number of Christians. Paul describes his own yearning to know Christ better and his own motivating hope in order to encourage others that this way of life is open to them as well. He then urges the other believers to be "thus minded" (Philippians 3:15). All believers have the same hope in Christ, for "there is one body, and one Spirit, even as ye are called in one hope of your calling" (Ephesians 4:4). All believers are indwelt by Christ, truly a mystery that the world cannot understand, "Christ in you, the hope of glory" (Colossians 1:27). Hope will affect how and what believers do in caring for souls.

Hope! The marvelous expectation that comes from faith in what God has promised for the future! Hope in Christ, in God's Word, and for all His promises brings courage, confidence, and comfort, even in the worst times because of God's trustworthy character. Biblical hope is not empty wishing, but solid expectation. This hope is "an anchor of the soul, both sure and stedfast" (Hebrews 6:19), because the "Lord Jesus Christ . . . is our hope" (1 Timothy 1:1). This is the "hope of eternal life, which God, that cannot lie, promised before the world began" (Titus 1:2). This hope is therefore intrinsically fixed on faith in God and His Word.

This hope is also based on God's love and presence through the Holy Spirit. Believers "rejoice in hope of the glory of God" (Romans 5:2). Hope instills confidence and a further outpouring of love. Paul declares that during difficult circumstances "hope maketh not ashamed; because the love of God is shed abroad in our hearts by the Holy Ghost which is given unto us" (Romans 5:5).

Faith, hope and love are all elements of the glorious Gospel. Paul says:

> We give thanks to God and the Father of our Lord Jesus Christ, praying always for you, Since we heard of your faith in Christ Jesus, and of the love which ye have to all the saints, For the hope which is laid up for you in heaven, whereof ye heard before in the word of the truth of the gospel; Which is come unto you, as it is in all the world; and bringeth forth fruit, as it doth also in you, since the day ye heard of it, and knew the grace of God in truth (Colossians 1:3-6).

In this section, Paul first offers thanks to God, because all that follows comes from His gracious hand.

Then we see a progression of spiritual activity. The truth of the Gospel brings forth faith in Christ Jesus, which in turn results in hope, in love for the saints, and in fruitfulness. As believers continue in faith, hope, and love, their lives are fruitful in daily service. They can remind one another of their hope of salvation, which is called a helmet because it protects the mind against onslaughts of the enemy, who wants to deceive believers into thinking that this present world is all there is (1 Thessalonians 5:8). Fellow believers can encourage one another in that hope laid up for them in heaven, not a self-indulging "pie in the sky by and by," but a solid inheritance consisting of reality that has far greater substance and holy essence than we can even comprehend. The Bible calls that eternal future *glory.*

Those who do not believe in the resurrection must fill their lives with temporal hope that has no real substance. If they have another hope beyond the grave other than Christ, they are deceived, and underneath their false hope lies terror. Indeed, without Christ they have no real hope. Before hearing and believing the Gospel, people are "without Christ, being aliens from the commonwealth of Israel, and strangers from the covenants of promise, having no hope, and without God in the world" (Ephesians 2:12).

But in Christ Jesus believers have hope of salvation, hope of righteousness by faith (Galatians 5:5), the hope of glory, the hope of eternal life (Titus 3:7), and the glorious hope of 1 John 3:2,3:

> Beloved, now are we the sons of God, and it doth not yet appear what we shall be: but we know that, when he shall appear, we shall be like him; for we shall see him as he is. And every man that hath this hope in him purifieth himself, even as he is pure.

As believers anticipate being eternally with Jesus and becoming like Him, their focus is on Him. Such hope actually purifies the believer before the fulfillment of the hope. That is because he is fixed on Christ and the goal set before him. Elsewhere we learn that we do become like Christ by gazing on His wonderful character: "But we all, with open face beholding as in a glass the glory of the Lord, are changed into the same image from glory to glory, even as by the Spirit of the Lord" (2 Corinthians 3:18).

Hope for Daily Living

The hope of the Gospel extends right into eternity, but it begins at the moment of salvation. This hope, which is grounded in God's Word, has an eternal future, but it gives strength and patience for daily living. God is intimately involved with every aspect of a believer's life. God may allow difficult circumstances to make the believer more like Christ, or He may allow difficult circumstances for purposes that extend beyond the believer. However, He has made certain promises that give hope to believers as they endure trials.

> There hath no temptation taken you but such as is common to man: but God is faithful, who will not suffer you to be tempted above that ye are able; but will with the temptation also make a way to escape, that ye may be able to bear it (1 Corinthians 10:13).

> The steps of a good man are ordered by the LORD: and he delighteth in his way. Though he fall, he shall not be utterly cast down: for the LORD upholdeth him with his hand (Psalm 37:23,24).

> But my God shall supply all your need according to his riches in glory by Christ Jesus (Philippians 4:19).

Besides the direct promises of God being a source of sound hope, believers are also to give hope to one another. They can offer hope in very practical matters when circumstances look hopeless. These offers of hope are more than words. In the Body of Christ believers should be able to hope for help and assistance when they are in troublesome circumstances.

A young couple with two young children suffering from a rapidly degenerating disease may have reached the end of their strength and patience if members of their church had not been there to assist them in holding and rocking the children, in bringing meals, and in just being there to help with whatever was needed. God worked through His children to give help and hope to the family. These young parents were not stranded in their efforts to deal with the situation. Instead, they were supported by the body in very practical ways. During this time of sharing hope through practical help, all who were involved grew in faith and patience.

As believers exercise hope in the Lord, they do develop patience (Romans 5:4; 8:25) and joy (Romans 12:12). Paul thanked God as he remembered the Thessalonian believers' "patience of hope" (1 Thessalonians 1:3). His instructions to the Romans gives a glimpse of how patience and hope from the Scriptures help believers to bear with one another:

> We then that are strong ought to bear the infirmities of the weak, and not to please ourselves. Let every one of us please his neighbour for his good to edification. For even Christ pleased not himself; but, as it is written, The reproaches of them that reproached thee fell on me. For whatsoever things were written aforetime were written for our learning, that we through patience and comfort of the scriptures might have hope. Now the God of patience and consolation grant you to be likeminded one toward another according to Christ Jesus: That ye may with one mind and one mouth glorify God, even the Father of our Lord Jesus Christ (Romans 15:1-6).

Hope helps believers to develop patience.

Ministering Hope

Besides motivating a believer to serve Christ, hope establishes the manner, the direction, and the content of ministering the care of souls.

> Now our Lord Jesus Christ himself, and God, even our Father, which hath loved us, and hath given us everlasting consolation and good hope through grace, Comfort your hearts, and stablish you in every good word and work (2 Thessalonians 2:16,17).

Believers who hope in Christ communicate that hope by how they conduct themselves as well as by what they say. Peter encourages believers who are suffering persecution to "sanctify the Lord God in your hearts: and be ready always to give an answer to every man that asketh you a reason of the hope that is in you with meekness and fear" (1 Peter 3:15). Such hope communicates that what they believe is worth believing.

Besides communicating quiet confidence, hope can cause believers to be bold in their witness for Christ, just as Paul wrote from prison:

> For I know that this shall turn to my salvation through your prayer, and the supply of the Spirit of Jesus Christ, According to my earnest expectation and my hope, that in nothing I shall be ashamed, but that with all boldness, as always, so now also Christ shall be magnified in my body, whether it be by life, or by death (Philippians 1:19,20).

As believers rejoice in hope, they desire to share that hope with unbelievers to bring them to a saving knowledge of Christ. Hope is given as the Gospel is preached, because salvation brings a living, enduring hope:

> Blessed be the God and Father of our Lord Jesus Christ, which according to his abundant mercy

hath begotten us again unto a lively hope by the resurrection of Jesus Christ from the dead, To an inheritance incorruptible, and undefiled, and that fadeth not away, reserved in heaven for you, Who are kept by the power of God through faith unto salvation ready to be revealed in the last time (1 Peter 1:3-5).

Can anyone offer such hope outside the Gospel of Jesus Christ? Truly believers have Good News for those around them. Their hope in Christ and the hope they can talk about can motivate them to testify when the Lord gives opportunities.

Just as Paul encouraged believers to hope in the Lord, so also are believers to encourage one another to "continue in the faith grounded and settled, and be not moved away from the hope of the gospel, which ye have heard" (Colossians 1:23). Believers have numerous opportunities to minister hope to one another as they themselves continue in hope.

Believers can also exhort one another to be diligent in hope just as Peter exhorts: "Wherefore gird up the loins of your mind, be sober, and hope to the end for the grace that is to be brought unto you at the revelation of Jesus Christ" (1 Peter 1:13). Or, as Hebrews says:

And we desire that every one of you do show the same diligence to the full assurance of hope unto the end: That ye be not slothful, but followers of them who through faith and patience inherit the promises (Hebrews 6:11,12).

Just as Paul prayed for believers to know, understand, and experience the hope of their calling, so also are believers to pray for one another.

Wherefore I also, after I heard of your faith in the Lord Jesus, and love unto all the saints, Cease not to give thanks for you, making mention of you in my prayers; That the God of our Lord Jesus Christ, the Father of glory, may give unto you the spirit of wisdom and revelation in the knowledge of him: The eyes of your understanding being enlightened; that ye may know what is the hope of his calling, and what the riches of the glory of his inheritance in the saints, And what is the exceeding greatness of his power to us-ward who believe, according to the working of his mighty power, Which he wrought in Christ, when he raised him from the dead, and set him at his own right hand in the heavenly places (Ephesians 1:15-20).

Praying for one another along the lines that Paul prayed and according to what God has promised to His children is one of the most effective means of ministering to one another in the Body of Christ. As believers pray for one another, the Lord works mightily to do His will. Just knowing that other believers are praying can be such a strong encouragement to one who is facing challenges. Hope can be rekindled through prayer.

Just reminding one another of the glorious hope God has given His children edifies the Body of Christ. Believers might bless one another with these words: "Now the God of hope fill you with all joy and peace in believing, that ye may abound in hope, through the power of the Holy Ghost" (Romans 15:13).

Moment by moment believers should be:

Looking for that blessed hope, and the glorious appearing of the great God and our Saviour Jesus Christ; Who gave himself for us, that he might redeem us from all iniquity, and purify unto himself a peculiar people, zealous of good works (Titus 2:13,14).

As you hope in the Lord, you will be competent to minister that same hope to one another.

10

Ministering Love to One Another

Has there ever been an era when people have loved themselves more than today? Perhaps it's just our culture. More likely it's the prophesied increase in the same desires of the flesh and mind that have pervaded the world since the first bite of forbidden fruit (2 Timothy 3:1-7). Yet, with all the glitz of so-called Christian entertainment and emulation of the world's glamour, there seems to be little difference between the church and the world. Polls of Christians reveal that Christians act nearly the same as unbelievers. How can this horrible trend be reversed? We contend that as believers return to their first love, take up their cross and follow Christ we will see change. As each believer participates in the mutual care of the Body of Christ, we will see a difference. Then, instead of encouraging

151

each other to love oneself more, believers will encourage one another to place Christ's interests above their own.

This chapter is written to encourage believers to minister with confidence—to continue to do what they may already be doing in the Body of Christ. Much of this will be a reminder of what believers already know to be true. However, in this era of self, we need to remind each other about these basic principles of love.

Just as at the advent of Christianity, believers are called to deny themselves and place God's interests above their own. Now is the time to turn away from the sirens of the world that tempt believers to live for themselves in self-indulgence, self-realization, self-satisfaction, and self-love. While there are yet many believers who do put Christ's interests above their own and who deny themselves and take up their cross daily, it nevertheless seems as if we have come to those perilous times Paul describes in his letter to Timothy.

> This know also, that in the last days perilous times shall come. For men shall be lovers of their own selves, covetous, boasters, proud, blasphemers, disobedient to parents, unthankful, unholy, Without natural affection, trucebreakers, false accusers, incontinent, fierce, despisers of those that are good, traitors, heady, highminded, lovers of pleasures more than lovers of God; Having a form of godliness, but denying the power thereof: from such turn away. For of this sort are they which creep into houses, and lead captive silly women laden with sins, led away with divers lusts, Ever learning, and never able to come to the knowledge of the truth (2 Timothy 3:1-7).

Paul's words sound as if he is speaking about our time. Every detail in the above description seems to increase daily. How can a few followers of Christ turn this situation around? As each one denies himself and resists the temptation to follow the worldly arguments for self-love, self-worth, and self-esteem, the first step is taken. Then, as each one in the Body of Christ seeks one another's good, the next step is taken, until by Christ's grace and power:

> . . . the whole body fitly joined together and compacted by that which every joint supplieth, according to the effectual working in the measure of every part, maketh increase of the body unto the edifying of itself in love" (Ephesians 4:16).

Self-seeking is not a new malady among those who call themselves Christians. In his letter to the Philippian church, Paul says, "For all seek their own, not the things which are Jesus Christ's" (Philippians 2:21). Believers who seek God's will above their own and who place the well being of others before their own can be used mightily by God for His glory. They will be ready to do the smallest or lowliest tasks and they will be prepared and equipped by the Lord to do what they would never be able to do by themselves. They will see God working in and through them and will marvel— but, not at themselves,

Loving God is not only the purest purpose, action, and passion; loving God changes the purpose, actions, and goal of everything a person does. Human beings organize their lives around what they love most, and their priorities often reveal their first love. When the Pharisees, who loved preeminence, attempted to trap Jesus with questions, Jesus took the opportunity to teach profound truths. When asked, "Master, which is the great commandment in the law?" Jesus answered:

> Thou shalt love the Lord thy God with all thy heart, and with all thy soul, and with all thy mind. This is the first and great commandment. And the second is like unto it, Thou shalt love thy neighbour as thyself. On these two commandments hang all the law and the prophets (Matthew 22:36-40).

The Great Commandment to "love the Lord thy God with all thy heart, and with all thy soul, and with all thy mind" is all-encompassing. If a person's entire inner being is devoted to loving God, godly actions will follow. Jesus reveals this when He says: "He that hath my commandments, and keepeth them, he it is that loveth me: and he that loveth me shall be loved of my Father, and I will love him, and will manifest myself to him" (John 14:21).

Luke records the final phrase to the Great Commandment: "and with all thy strength" (Luke 10:27). This is not a love expressed casually or when the mood is right or when it's convenient. The commandment is not asking for anything half-hearted.

God's grace enables believers to follow both "the first and great commandment" and the second, which "is like unto it, Thou shalt love thy neighbour as thyself." John writes about God's love empowering believers to love.

> Beloved, let us love one another: for love is of God; and every one that loveth is born of God, and knoweth God. He that loveth not knoweth not God; for God is love. In this was manifested the love of God toward us, because that God sent his only begotten Son into the world, that we might live through him. Herein is love, not that we loved God, but that he loved us, and sent his Son to be the propitiation for our sins (1 John 4:7-10).

God loved first and is the source of all true love. He is the source of love for every believer. Love flows from God to the believer, out to others and back to God. But, love that is directed inward to self can stagnate. It is no longer fresh and flowing.

As believers empty out their supply of love by loving God and others, their supply is replenished. But, if love is hoarded, there is no fresh supply. Therefore, teachings that encourage Christians to love themselves are at cross-purposes with the very intent of God's love. Indeed, people already do love themselves. Jesus says to love others "as thyself." The entire thrust of the New Testament is to love God and others, especially brothers and sisters in Christ: "A new commandment I give unto you, That ye love one another; as I have loved you, that ye also love one another" (John 13:34). This kind of love goes beyond feelings and even kindness. Jesus' love went to the Cross. His love is sacrificial, and He inspires and empowers believers to love one another sacrificially, because He is in them and they are in Him.

Love is the identifying mark of Christians. Jesus said, "By this shall all men know that ye are my disciples, if ye have love one to another" (John 13:35). Not only is love the evidence of one's faith; it is the normal result of God dwelling in a person.

> Beloved, if God so loved us, we ought also to love one another. No man hath seen God at any time. If we love one another, God dwelleth in us, and his love is perfected in us (1 John 4:11,12).

One does not perfect love for others through self-effort. One does so through responding to God's love, because it is God's love that is perfected in believers.

Humanistic Love

Even though he is now deceased, Carl Rogers is still one of the best-known and most-admired psychologists in the world. The most important principle Rogers "discovered" during his lifetime of studying human behavior and practicing psychotherapy was that of "love between persons," which he considered to be his crowning discovery. When Rogers abandoned Christianity while in seminary and turned his devotion to humanistic psychology, he lost sight of biblical love. While his "discovery" may seem important from a limited, worldly view, it is a far cry from the love found in God's Word. Rogers "love between persons" was limited to natural human love, which is often merely an extension of self-love. Jesus reveals the shortcoming of human love in Matthew 5:46,47.

> For if ye love them which love you, what reward have ye? do not even the publicans the same? And if ye salute your brethren only, what do ye more than others? do not even the publicans so?

Rogers ignored the divine source of love, disregarded the great commandment to "love the Lord thy God," and failed to mention God's love for mankind. What is shocking is to hear pastors, who should know God's love, say they didn't really know what love was until they read Rogers. But, Rogers' "love between persons" was to help one feel self-worth. It was not sacrificial love that went to the Cross to redeem sinners.

Christian Love

Christian love is far greater than human love. Jesus points out the difference between natural human love and His kind of love when he says:

> But I say unto you, Love your enemies, bless them that curse you, do good to them that hate you, and pray for them which despitefully use you, and persecute you; That ye may be the children of your Father which is in heaven: for he maketh his sun to rise on the evil and on the good, and sendeth rain on the just and on the unjust. For if ye love them which love you, what reward have ye? do not even the publicans the same? (Matthew 5:44-46).

John continues with more statements about the kind of love that comes from dwelling in God and being indwelt by God. Believers grow in faith as their knowledge of God's love increases (1 John 4:16). They discover this reality: "There is no fear in love; but perfect love casteth out fear" (1 John 4:18).

Love in the Body of Christ

Because God is love, all interactions among believers within the Body of Christ are to be motivated by love, expressed in love, and acted in love.

> We love him, because he first loved us. If a man
> say, I love God, and hateth his brother, he is a liar:
> for he that loveth not his brother whom he hath
> seen, how can he love God whom he hath not seen?
> And this commandment have we from him, That
> he who loveth God love his brother also (1 John
> 4:19-21).

However, godly love is not sugar-coated niceness to
one another. It is genuine concern that will not depart
from truth. Believers are called to speak the truth in
love (Ephesians 4:15). They are called to admonish one
another. The Body is even called to discipline and to
disfellowship members for biblical reasons. Such is to be
done out of love for God and the brethren and for the
purpose of restoration and reconciliation. True love may
be stern as well as gentle. Jesus was stern to the Pharisees, but His purpose was to reveal truth that they
might repent.

How is this love for God and one another to be
worked out in daily life? The New Testament is filled
with descriptions of how believers are to relate to one
another. One excellent passage is found in Paul's letter
to the Colossian believers. The third chapter reminds
believers of their identify in Christ and how their position in Him and the promise of a glorious eternity with
Him should change their desires and motives.

> If ye then be risen with Christ, seek those things
> which are above, where Christ sitteth on the right
> hand of God. Set your affection on things above,
> not on things on the earth. For ye are dead, and
> your life is hid with Christ in God. When Christ,
> who is our life, shall appear, then shall ye also
> appear with him in glory (Colossians 3:1-4).

As believers identify with Christ they reckon themselves dead to the old life and realize Christ as being
their life. How essential it is for believers to find their
identity in Christ, because that is the essence of their

present life. "Therefore if any man be in Christ, he is a new creature: old things are passed away; behold, all things are become new" (2 Corinthians 5:17). That is why it is both pointless and sinful for believers to attempt to fix their lives by going back into their faulty memories of the past. The past life is to be reckoned dead. The believer now has a new life, not just a new beginning, but new life in Christ.

Then, because of their relationship with Christ, believers are no longer to live according to the old ways of the world and the flesh.

> Mortify therefore your members which are upon the earth; fornication, uncleanness, inordinate affection, evil concupiscence, and covetousness, which is idolatry: For which things' sake the wrath of God cometh on the children of disobedience: In the which ye also walked some time, when ye lived in them. But now ye also put off all these; anger, wrath, malice, blasphemy, filthy communication out of your mouth. Lie not one to another, seeing that ye have put off the old man with his deeds (Colossians 3:5-9).

If any believer is living according to the above description, he knows that he is not living according to the new life in Christ. He has reverted back to the old life, which is to be reckoned dead and put off. As soon as a believer recognizes he is not living according to the new life, he is to turn back to the Lord and confess his sin. "If we confess our sins, he is faithful and just to forgive us our sins, and to cleanse us from all unrighteousness" (1 John 1:9). Christians sin when they fail to live according to Christ in them. Every time they turn back to the Lord, they mortify the flesh and put on "the new man, which is renewed in knowledge after the image of him that created him" (Colossians 3:10).

The new man believers put on is their life in Christ. This new life is shared equally by all believers, because in Him there are no worldly distinctions such as race, culture, economics, or position in life (Colossians 3: 10,11). In Christ, loving one another applies to all believers.

Paul enumerates some ways in which believers love one another when they "have put on the new man."

> Put on therefore, as the elect of God, holy and beloved, bowels of mercies, kindness, humbleness of mind, meekness, longsuffering; Forbearing one another, and forgiving one another, if any man have a quarrel against any: even as Christ forgave you, so also do ye. And above all these things put on charity, which is the bond of perfectness (Colossians 3:12-14).

Such putting on happens on the inside: "bowels of mercies, kindness, humbleness of mind, meekness, longsuffering." These are all inner attitudes and attributes of Christ. Every time believers put on Christ, they put on His attitudes and attributes. Every time they act according to Christ's attitudes and attributes, they are mortifying the flesh, walking according to the Spirit, and bearing fruit. With such inner transformation, they put up with each other and forgive one another.

To "put on charity" means to love one another in a selfless manner that seeks the welfare of others and looks for opportunities to serve. This is not a superficial putting on as one might put on a happy face. This is putting on the essence of Christ's love and acting accordingly.

> Charity suffereth long, and is kind; charity envieth not; charity vaunteth not itself, is not puffed up, Doth not behave itself unseemly, seeketh not her own, is not easily provoked, thinketh no evil; Rejoiceth not in iniquity, but rejoiceth in the truth; Beareth all things, believeth all things, hopeth all things, endureth all things (1 Corinthians 13:4-7).

Love is described both by what it is and what it is
not. Love does not seek to have one's own way. Godly
love is not selfish in any way. Nor is there any room for
pride. Godly love is humble, sacrificial, and gracious.
And, at the same time, Godly love never departs from
truth. Its source is Christ and includes both grace and
truth (John 1:17).

As believers put on Christ they are able to let God's
peace rule their hearts and govern their actions, all the
while being thankful. Moreover the "word of Christ" is
to dwell in them "richly in all wisdom." But even here,
they are not to keep His Word to themselves or horde
God's wisdom. No, they are to both teach and admonish
one another. Notice that this letter is addressed to the
whole church at Colosse. This means that all believers
share to some degree in the teaching and admonishing.
Here is the flow of love and help to one another for
every member of the Body of Christ to grow into His
likeness.

> And let the peace of God rule in your hearts, to the
> which also ye are called in one body; and be ye
> thankful. Let the word of Christ dwell in you
> richly in all wisdom; teaching and admonishing
> one another in psalms and hymns and spiritual
> songs, singing with grace in your hearts to the
> Lord. And whatsoever ye do in word or deed, do all
> in the name of the Lord Jesus, giving thanks to
> God and the Father by him (Colossians 3:15-17).

Nothing is left out here, because the final statement
covers every word and every deed—all to be done "in
the name of the Lord Jesus, giving thanks to God and
the Father by him." Just think what would happen if all
who profess Christ took these words seriously and lived
by them according to the very life of Christ in them.

One Anothers in the Body of Christ

There is plenty of information in the New Testament
about how the Body of Christ is to function. There is a

wealth of information in the letters to the churches about how Christians are to care for one another. Believers are not without information and instruction. Neither are they without resources to care for one another and help one another grow in the Lord. The average believer already knows as much as he needs to mutually care for fellow believers.

Without being noticed, many believers are already ministering to fellow believers. However, as believers become confident in their ability in Christ and recognize their responsibility to His Body, mutual care will increase to the edification of the Body for the glory of God. The following is merely a glimpse of how Christians may care for one another.

1. Love one another. "This is my commandment, That ye love one another, as I have loved you" (John 15:12). Christ loved to the uttermost, to the Cross. Love in the Body of Christ is not simply a feeling of affection. It is an inner attitude that will result in actions for the good of others. This love is more than simply a passive attitude of wishing well for the other person; it is earnest and fervent. "Seeing ye have purified your souls in obeying the truth through the Spirit unto unfeigned love of the brethren, see that ye love one another with a pure heart fervently" (1 Peter 1:22) Fervent love involves striving to the uttermost for the good of a fellow believer. Such earnest and fervent love is one that puts the good of another before self and will care so much that it will warn, exhort, and even rebuke a fellow believer for the purpose of restoration. Such is not a pleasant task, but if it is necessary, a believer who loves will risk loss for the sake of one soul repenting and being restored (James 5:19-20). There are numerous verses that instruct believers to love one another.

2. Be kind to one another. "Be kindly affectioned one to another with brotherly love; in honour preferring one another" (Romans 12:10). Here even the emotions are commanded as well as the actions, for if one is "kindly affectioned" to another person, he will work for the good of the other person. Kindness would be expressed in practical actions as well as in attitudes and words. In this same verse believers are instructed to prefer one another, that is, to put the other person first. This is similar to Philippians 2:3: "Let nothing be done through strife or vainglory; but in lowliness of mind let each esteem other better than themselves."

When people strive to excel in certain talents, they may become competitive and even envious of others who are being successful. A fairly new believer spoke glowing words about a singer in the church. The response of her Christian friend, who was also a singer, was enthusiastic agreement.

The new believer was surprised and asked, "Aren't you jealous?"

The friend answered, "Of course not."

The new believer pressed the issue, but the woman replied, "Why should I not rejoice that God has gifted a sister in Christ and is using her for His glory? Her excellent singing voice does not lessen the gift God has given me. I really do rejoice in the gift He has given her. Christ is glorified and the body is edified."

3. Forgive one another. "And be ye kind one to another, tenderhearted, forgiving one another, even as God for Christ's sake hath forgiven you" (Ephesians 4:32). Kindness extends the same mercy and forgiveness that Christ provided for believers. Without forgiveness, kindness may only last as long as everything goes one's way. When believers truly express the kindness and forgiveness of Christ, they die to self, because they put Christ and His will for others before their own apparent needs and desires.

Forgiveness is the choice and promise not to hold the sin against the offender any longer. It is a loving response of one who is indwelt by God and who desires Jesus' life to be manifest through him. Forgiveness accepts the pain of the offense and relinquishes the right to retaliation, bitterness, or resentment. Forgiveness begins in the inner person with an attitude ready to forgive the offender, should he confess and repent. Such an attitude of forgiveness prevents bitterness and resentment, but it does not prevent one from trying to make a situation right through confronting a fellow believer in love.

Unforgiveness takes its toll in poor relationships. It keeps both the unforgiving and the unforgiven in bondage to the offense. People who complain about communication problems may be harboring unforgiveness. Unforgiveness creates barriers between people and also alienates people from God. Bitterness hardens the heart from receiving God's love as well as the love of other people.

Forgiveness also places trust in God to deal with both the offender and the results of the offense. Forgiveness releases both the forgiver and the forgiven one from a relationship of blame, retaliation, bitterness, and resentment. The choice to forgive releases the flow of God's love.

Love is also expressed through admitting and confessing sin when we have wronged others. Asking forgiveness from a fellow believer gives that person the opportunity to forgive. Admitting wrong and asking forgiveness is often far more difficult and far more humiliating than extending forgiveness. However, in many cases confession of wrong opens the way for the other person to confess so that mutual forgiveness and healing may occur. In asking forgiveness, it is wise to verbally admit having wronged the person and then specifically to ask, "Will you forgive me?" Just saying, "I'm sorry," is not enough because it does not include the confession or the request.

4. Forbearing one another in love. One great form of kindness is that which is expressed when others in the Body are irritating. Notice how Paul instructs believers to treat one another: "With all lowliness and meekness, with longsuffering, forbearing one another in love" (Ephesians 4:2). This is putting up with people who may be insufferable "with all lowliness and meekness, with longsuffering," which is a graphic way to express the idea of patience, because patience suffers long.

Consider the most difficult person in your life and think of being yoked together with that person and what forbearance that would take. Then remember that Christ has called each believer to be yoked together with Him. In His invitation to take His yoke upon us and learn of Him, He speaks of being "meek and lowly in heart" (Matthew 11:28-30). Believers are yoked with Christ and they are connected to each other because all are part of one Body. Therefore, believers need to tolerate being close to others who are also in the process of sanctification "with all lowliness and meekness, with longsuffering, forbearing one another in love."

5. Exhort one another. Another ministry to one another in the Body of Christ is exhortation. Hebrews 3:13 says, "But exhort one another daily, while it is called To day; lest any of you be hardened through the deceitfulness of sin." Exhorting is strongly urging or making a strong persuasive appeal to motivate a fellow believer to do God's will. Hebrews 10:24 uses an even stronger word—*provoke*. "And let us consider one another to provoke unto love and good works."

Because of the priesthood of all believers, exhortation is not to be limited to formal teaching and preaching. Exhorting one another is exercising mutual care, as the next verse says: "Not forsaking the assembling of ourselves together, as the manner of some is; but exhorting one another: and so much the more, as ye see the day approaching" (Hebrews 10:25). If believers are to exhort one another, it is understood that they are also willing to be recipients of exhortation in all humility with wisdom, checking the Scriptures to see whether the exhortation is from God (Acts 17:1; 1 John 4:1).

6. Teaching one another. "Let the word of Christ dwell in you richly in all wisdom; teaching and admonishing one another in psalms and hymns and spiritual songs, singing with grace in your hearts to the Lord"

(Colossians 3:16). Believers whose minds are influenced and occupied with God's Word have much to give one another regarding wisdom, instruction, and warning. As Christians fill their hearts and minds with Scripture, they have a treasure from which to draw.

> A good man out of the good treasure of his heart bringeth forth that which is good; and an evil man out of the evil treasure of his heart bringeth forth that which is evil: for of the abundance of the heart his mouth speaketh (Luke 6:45).

Those who are converted and thereby indwelt by Christ Jesus have been given His righteousness, and as they fill their hearts and minds with Scripture, they are competent to minister. Believers are equipped to teach and admonish one another. Paul says: "And I myself also am persuaded of you, my brethren, that ye also are full of goodness, filled with all knowledge, able also to admonish one another" (Romans 15:14). Again, this statement is addressed to the entire church, not just a few who might consider themselves "counselors." They are able to admonish each other, because they are filled with both goodness and knowledge, because of Christ in them and because of their diligence in continuing in His Word.

7. Admonishing one another. The word *admonish* has to do with warning through instruction. For instance, in Proverbs 5-7 the young man is warned concerning those who might entice him to do evil.

Admonishing calls for humility and graciousness. Love does not have or express an arrogant attitude. Instead, when believers admonish one another they must remember their own weaknesses and their utter dependence on Christ. On two occasions when Paul wrote about his ministry as an Apostle, he also referred to himself as a sinner. Paul's calling was high, but he always remembered from whence Christ saved him (1 Timothy 1:12-15).

Teaching and admonishing require listening. As one speaks the other listens. If believers are teaching and admonishing one another, there is godly conversation with each speaking that which edifies the other (Ephesians 4:29). And let the other listen attentively to learn.

> A wise man will hear, and will increase learning; and a man of understanding shall attain unto wise counsels: To understand a proverb, and the interpretation; the words of the wise, and their dark sayings. The fear of the LORD is the beginning of knowledge: but fools despise wisdom and instruction (Proverbs 1:5-7).

A rebellious, prideful heart resists admonishing, but a wise person will listen to admonishing (instruction with warning) and will go to the Lord and to His Word to determine whether the admonishing is on target.

> Reprove not a scorner, lest he hate thee: rebuke a wise man, and he will love thee. Give instruction to a wise man, and he will be yet wiser: teach a just man, and he will increase in learning (Proverbs 9:8,9).

There will be people in the church who want help but who do not actually want the full scope of Christianity. These individuals want help without truly believing or trusting God. They want God to improve their circumstances without disturbing their flesh. When Jesus ministered healing and mercy, the crowds eagerly received. They pursued Him to receive more material blessings after He fed the five thousand. But when He said He was the bread of heaven and that to have life they would have to eat His flesh and drink His blood— to receive and believe Him and to live in a dependent relationship to Him—many departed.

Although many people eagerly received the teachings and counsel of Jesus, there came a time when His followers were given the choice to deny themselves, take up the cross, and follow Him. He recognized that not all people would receive His love and His Word. When ministry is both given and received, the speaker speaks the truth in love and the listener responds in truth and love. In such a way the whole Body is edified.

8. Comfort one another. After Paul reminds believers of their glorious future, he says, "Wherefore comfort yourselves together, and edify one another, even as also ye do" (1 Thessalonians 5:11). Reminding one another of the truth of the Gospel and about all the Lord has said in His Word brings great comfort to believers. Every believer is competent to comfort, encourage, and edify one another in the Body of Christ with the truth and comfort of God (2 Corinthians 1:3,4).

9. Submitting to one another. Paul speaks of Christians: "Submitting yourselves one to another in the fear of God" (Ephesians 5:21). Mutual care in the Body of Christ requires mutual submission. Both the one who gives and the one who receives must submit to one another. This submission is often expressed in listening to what the other person has to say, as when one teaches, encourages, exhorts, or admonishes a fellow believer. Both speak; both listen; both submit to one another in the process.

Submission in mutual care is especially important when hospitality is given. If, for instance a person needs a place to live for a space of time and another believer comes alongside to supply that need, the recipient must in all graciousness submit to the authority of the household for the duration of the stay. On the other hand, the person who extends such hospitality should treat the guest with all respect. Mutual submission brings order and grace.

10. Serving one another. "For, brethren, ye have been called unto liberty; only use not liberty for an occasion to the flesh, but by love serve one another" (Galatians 5:13). Giving love by serving one another leaves much room for creativity. The field is wide open. How may I serve my spouse, my children, my pastor, my fellow believer? There are millions of possibilities, but we need to know one another and love one another to know how and when to serve.

Serving one another by love means that all service comes under biblical guidelines. For instance, there are some Christians who are so busy serving believers outside their own family that their family suffers. Those who serve one another need to prioritize whom the Lord would have them serve. To neglect one's own children, but teach a Sunday school class of other people's children would certainly be an example of misplaced service. Prayerfully prioritizing one's service in the Body of Christ will help meet all needs and also help involve fellow believers who otherwise might not serve.

When we directed a personal care ministry in a local church, we informed those on the list to help that a "no" answer was as valuable as a "yes" answer if they had prayed about whether or not to take on the task. We firmly believed that God had someone for each task and that if one person did not do the work God had another in mind, who might otherwise not have the opportunity to serve. After all, serving one another is a privilege given by God's grace whereby we may actively participate in His Body and glorify Him in the process.

Serving one another often involves sharing our belongings. This is an area where wisdom and spiritual discernment are needed, because there are those who take advantage of Christians' willingness to give. We know pastors who have given money to people who told heart-wrenching stories, only to learn later that they'd been swindled. That is why believers need to know one another to serve one another, especially in giving funds. That is also why these gifts are to be operating among believers in the local fellowship. In some instances it is better to supply goods or services rather than to give money. Even here, the Scripture provides loving guidelines:

For even when we were with you, this we commanded you, that if any would not work, neither should he eat. For we hear that there are some which walk among you disorderly, working not at all, but are busybodies. Now them that are such we command and exhort by our Lord Jesus Christ, that with quietness they work, and eat their own bread (2 Thessalonians 3:10-12).

The whole counsel of God gives wisdom and discernment for giving, serving, admonishing, and ministering to one another.

11. Receiving one another. "Wherefore receive ye one another, as Christ also received us to the glory of God" (Romans 15:7). *Receive* is the opposite of *reject.* Such receiving in fellowship should discourage cliques, which so easily develop among immature Christians. The word *receive* here suggests welcoming and even taking a special interest in one another. The same idea is expressed at the end of Paul's letter to the Romans: "Salute one another with an holy kiss. The churches of Christ salute you" (Romans 16:16). Are such words formalities at the end of a letter, or are they truly meant to encourage believers to welcome one another with expressions of fellowship and belonging? Believers often forget that genuine interest and welcome can be expressions of Christ's love and a reminder that we belong to the same Lord and therefore to each other. Although we may be rejected in the world, we are to welcome one another with genuine regard.

Loving One Another Expresses Our Love for God

This chapter is just a glimpse of ways Christians are called to express their love for one another. Moreover, all love for another is an expression of our love for God. John says:

Beloved, if God so loved us, we ought also to love one another. No man hath seen God at any time. If we love one another, God dwelleth in us, and his love is perfected in us (1 John 4:11-12).

Paul emphasizes the stellar importance of biblical love, when he says at the end of 1 Corinthians 13, "And now abideth faith, hope, charity, these three; but the greatest of these is charity." Believers actively love God and one another as they participate in the mutual care of one another in the Body of Christ. The Body is edified and God is glorified.

11

Ministering Mercy and Truth

Presenting the way of the Lord, as revealed by the Word of God and the Holy Spirit, includes both the manner of presentation and the content of conversation. The conversation of biblical care calls for a combination of mercy and truth and a balance of listening and speaking.

Because God desires to draw persons closer to Himself through love, biblical care must be given in love. Yet God's love includes truth as well.

> Let not mercy and truth forsake thee: bind them about thy neck; write them upon the table of thine heart: So shalt thou find favour and good understanding in the sight of God and man (Proverbs 3:3-4).

The Bible does not teach a methodology of merely reflecting a person's feelings, or one of shallow sentimentality, or one of autocratic severity. The Bible teaches, through countless illustrations and principles, that there must be both mercy and truth. Any ministry that lacks this combination will fall short of the Bible's standard.

Scripture is firm and unchanging in principle. Yet, mutual care in the Body of Christ is not rigid. Jesus did not minister in an identical way to all individuals. He met each person where he was without lowering the standard. In so doing, Jesus revealed the perfect combination of mercy and truth. In wisdom Jesus presented truth and justice in the manner most effective for each particular person. When the rich young ruler came to Jesus, Jesus ministered truth in mercy when He said that to follow God the young man would have to sell all he had. But without changing the standard, Jesus had a different message for Nicodemus: the need to be born again. If these messages had been reversed, there would not have been a perfect combination of mercy and truth.

Believers are called to give mercy and speak truth. Building up one another in the Body of Christ is participating in a creative process. God molds people with hands of love. Although truth requires change, God in His mercy never works more rapidly than an individual can tolerate. The Lord is gentle and compassionate. A believer who draws along side to help will want to reflect the Lord. Within an environment of mercy and concern and with the sure Word of truth, a believer who is suffering from problems of living may venture to learn, change, and grow. Before Jesus raised Lazarus from the dead, He taught truth to Martha, wept with Mary, and urged Martha to a greater level of faith. In aptly joining mercy with truth, patience with exhortation, and listening with teaching, one who ministers care will need to rely continually on the Holy Spirit for wisdom.

Mercy is extremely important. However, mercy exercised in the flesh may become mere sentimentality. Mercy not tempered by truth may take on the sufferings of others without leading them out of their suffering. As soon as a believer takes on the sinful feelings of a fellow believer (such as anger, bitterness, or hostility), he becomes part of the problem rather than part of God's answer. Such attitudes hinder the work of the Holy Spirit. Instead, the one who ministers God's grace seeks to maintain an attitude of meekness, kindness, mercy, and concern, undergirded by great faith in God.

On the other hand, much damage has been done through exercising exhortation without mercy and instruction. Those seeking help may be turned off before they are ready to turn God's way. Exhortation without mercy, exercised in the flesh, may lead to severe dogmatism. Unbalanced exhortation may also reveal a critical attitude that will interfere with the effective care of souls. One who exhibits dogmatism, a critical attitude, and the tendency to snap out quick orders from the Bible merely adds to the condemnation and may even promote rebellion.

When exhortation includes both mercy and careful instruction, an individual is encouraged to make right choices. One person may receive direct instruction and be motivated to change. But another may need encouragement to be motivated. If a person understands what he is doing correctly, he will be encouraged to continue in the right direction and be ready for further instruction. A fellow believer may stimulate another to continue a path of thinking and behaving. He may point out certain good actions or situations arising from the new patterns to encourage the person to continue God's way. Encouragement may sometimes be general but at other times be quite specific. The general prompting of another believer to discover God's will and to follow His ways is a constant attitude and activity in mutual care. Specific urging may be reserved for encouraging one to take important actions one may hesitate to begin.

An individual needs truth to be set free from past bondages in thinking, feeling, and acting. Therefore, within the supportive relationship of mercy, the one who comes alongside will teach truth and may strongly urge a fellow believer to obey the truth.

> Brethren, if any of you do err from the truth, and one convert him; Let him know, that he which converteth the sinner from the error of his way shall save a soul from death, and shall hide a multitude of sins (James 5:19-20).

Each era struggles between the extremities of laxity (mercy without truth) and legalism (truth without mercy). Earlier eras were characterized by legalism; now we are in an era characterized by laxity. What is needed today is a combination of mercy and truth based on God's Word.

An excellent example of truth and mercy extended to an individual without condoning sin can be seen in John 8:1-11. When the scribes and Pharisees brought to Jesus a woman who had been caught in the act of adultery, they demanded a response in order to trick Him. But Jesus demonstrated the love of God, which transforms lives. He gave everyone the opportunity to examine his own life in the light of God's Law when He said, "He that is without sin among you, let him first cast a stone at her." Then as Jesus wrote on the ground, they, "being convicted by their own conscience, went out one by one, beginning at the eldest, even unto the last: and Jesus was left alone, and the woman standing in the midst." Jesus motivated them to examine themselves so that each might be convicted in his own conscience. During this time the woman's conscience surely convicted her. She knew she was guilty, for Jesus said to her, "Neither do I condemn thee: go, and sin no more."

Jesus gave the woman both mercy and truth, for although He did not condemn her He did admonish her to change her behavior. She went away forgiven, ready to change. Without departing from truth or from the

Father's standard of righteousness, Jesus was caring, forgiving, and strengthening in His response to her. He loved and cared enough to give the amount of truth she could receive within the context of love. Believers need to be faithful to the whole counsel of God. If they give one another only the words that are easy and acceptable, they may remain weak and spiritually stagnant.

The comfort of mercy

Sometimes when a person has experienced loss or when he is going through difficult trials, the believer who comes alongside will not instruct, but simply minister the comfort of the Lord.

> Blessed be God, even the Father of our Lord Jesus Christ, the Father of mercies, and the God of all comfort; Who comforteth us in all our tribulation, that we may be able to comfort them which are in any trouble, by the comfort wherewith we ourselves are comforted of God (2 Corinthians 1:3-4).

Comfort from God eases grief and brings strength and hope. Often a fellow believer who has experienced similar loss or trials will be able to give greater comfort than one who has not yet lived through the experience. Nevertheless, nearly every Christian has encountered enough losses and problems of one sort or another to have discovered the comfort only God can give. Such comfort will lead to peace, healing, and renewed strength. But one should avoid commiserating with a person who chooses to remain in grief rather than to move toward receiving God's comfort and life. God uses His comfort to accomplish growth, change, and new strength.

When a Christian goes through a time of great change or difficult adjustment in life he may need a fellow believer to go through it with him. These times include such life adjustments as the death of a loved one, divorce, loss of health, loss of a job, and certain types of family problems. In such situations the fellow believer helps mainly by listening, identifying with the loss, and giving emotional and especially spiritual support. Moreover, that friend in Christ sensitively offers hope and encouragement for the future. He attempts to focus the eyes upon Jesus and the eternal promises of the Bible. This can only be done gently in faith. It is like applying oil to the wound. If a person tries to push hope and faith without identifying with compassion and love, he may cause the wound to smart, as though he had applied vinegar instead of oil.

Listening for truth in mercy

In godly conversation all participants listen to love, learn, and grow. The one who has come alongside to help listens with mercy to identify with the person seeking help, to understand what he is experiencing, and to express the love and concern of God. Such listening is more than empathic listening, however. It is not just for the one seeking help to "get it all out" so that he will somehow be relieved, but rather for all participants to learn from God's Word.

Responsive listening involves the heart, mind, eyes, and body, as well as the ears. It is an attitude that originates from a loving heart. Just by listening, one can communicate respect, concern, and love. As one listens to the words being spoken by the other person, he is, at the same time, considering God's great love, concern, wisdom, and power to help.

The listener's response is often the loudest statement he makes. For instance, when someone confesses some lurid sin, a reaction of righteous indignation, shock, or morbid curiosity would not establish a good ministry atmosphere. On the other hand, a response of concern for the spiritual welfare of the one who has sinned and of patience and meekness (quiet strength without a hint of superiority) can establish a haven for spiritual transformation.

The helper can hold certain truths in mind while the fellow believer is confessing devastating sin: What is being said right now is crucially important to this individual. God loves him and has a way out of this destruction. A confession like this is not strange to God's ears, though He grieves for His child who has sinned and is ready to minister mercy, grace, forgiveness, and truth to transform him. Such confession prepares a person to turn away from sin towards the Lord and His way. The person seeking help needs someone who can listen without fear and who can point to God's way out of the problems.

Compassionate listening prepares the climate for truth. Careful listening helps one determine what areas of truth may need to be explored or emphasized. The Bible speaks of the value of listening for truth: "He that answereth a matter before he heareth it, it is folly and shame unto him" (Proverbs 18:13). Through thoughtful listening one can gain necessary information and provide an accurate perspective.

Wise listening can help a caring believer to find out information and gain clarity in areas of confusion. Even then it may be difficult to find out what is really going on. In one study of patients receiving psychotherapy, it was discovered that "forty percent of [the patients] admitted that they were withholding information from their therapists."[1] At a day-long symposium at Columbia University, "the psychoanalytic relationship was seen as a prime example of how human communication can depend on lies."[2] Although any conversation should be honest, many are not.

Besides withholding information and deliberately lying, people communicate what they believe to be true from their limited and sometimes biased position. One therefore cannot always depend on receiving accurate information. Proverbs 18:17 says: "He that is first in his own cause seemeth just; but his neighbour cometh and searcheth him." In caring for souls, one must be cautious in listening to a person's explanations or descriptions of situations. Discriminating listening involves careful attention and pertinent questions. "The heart of the prudent getteth knowledge; and the ear of the wise seeketh knowledge" (Proverbs 18:15). Still, God is the only One who truly understands and knows about an individual and his circumstances. That is why those who minister the care of souls assist fellow believers to find help from God and His Word. The purpose of biblical conversation should always be to move people closer to God.

Whether a listener understands what an individual is really saying or whether he just thinks he understands is an area of concern that can be dealt with through questions of clarification and attempts to restate what the other person has said. In trying to communicate a feeling or deep inner response to a situation or a complex network of circumstances, the speaker is limited to the vocabulary of ordinary language. To further compound the problem, words carry emotional overtones and subtle variations of meaning. There is a strong temptation for a listener to act as though he understands, when he may not understand at all. A good listener will check to see if he is grasping what is meant. He will also need to rely on the Lord to bring understanding.

Questions stimulating clear thinking and perception can be extremely beneficial in opening ways of thinking and behaving according to God's truth. Such attention also tends to make the speaker more responsible for what he says. Quite often people fall into a pattern of letting hurtful remarks slip out without the least sense of concern. By providing focus through questions, a care giver can also prevent rambling and repetition. Rather than just going on and on or talking in circles, the conversation can move in the direction of restoration, change, or a new course of action.

Questions of clarification are useful in conversation for change. All participants need a clear focus; all need discernment and wisdom. As the one giving care listens objectively and asks questions, the other may begin to see the nature of his problem more clearly and may discover answers. Furthermore, when a fellow believer has listened and sought to understand, the one seeking help is more receptive to consider what might be said during the conversation.

Teaching Truth in Mercy

As important as listening is within a ministry context, listening alone is usually not enough. Careful instruction and guidance through practical application of biblical principles are often necessary for change. The care of souls includes private Bible instruction. Biblical ministry involves the whole counsel of God, because only God knows what is really needed at the moment as well as in the future. Both a working knowledge of Scripture and the active presence of the Holy Spirit are essential in every biblical conversation for change.

Teaching principles from God's Word will be interwoven throughout the conversation. Since all believers need to learn how to live more effectively according to God's design, practical suggestions as to how and what to change should grow out of God's Word. Since the Holy Spirit speaks effectively through the Bible, the spiritual care giver will rely on the Bible as his primary source book. Paul's wise advice applies to the personal care of souls as well as to preaching:

> I charge thee therefore before God, and the Lord Jesus Christ, who shall judge the quick and the dead at his appearing and his kingdom; Preach the word; be instant in season, out of season; reprove, rebuke, exhort with all longsuffering and doctrine (2 Timothy 4:1,2).

Notice the source and manner of instruction. The teaching is based on God's Word, includes correction and encouragement. It is given in kindness and patience. Correction can only be accomplished effectively in love with great respect for the individual. When rebuke is necessary, there needs to be careful instruction as to how one might change or do things differently.

Whenever the Lord points out error, He also shows the right way. Rather than condemnation there is hope and help for change. Often correction can be given as an alternative plan of action or behavior. When someone truly sees that choices are available and recognizes that certain alternatives agree with God's will for him, he will not see such correction as criticism, but rather as hope.

Each Christian is in the process of being recreated (Romans 12:1,2; Ephesians). He is vulnerable and he is precious. Therefore, those who minister in the care of souls should seek God's wisdom in determining which biblical actions need to be encouraged and which errors call for attention. The obvious errors may not be the first ones the Lord will correct. As one becomes a willing learner, he is ready to see possibilities for change and growth. He will begin to pay attention to the Lord. He will check his attitudes, thoughts, words, and actions with Scripture to see if he is thinking and acting according to the life of Jesus in him or according to the ways of the flesh.

When believers minister to one another, they need to remember that what they say may include both biblical truth and human interpretation and application. The one giving care should encourage biblical principles and teach biblical truth, but he should not be dogmatic about practical application. Applications may be suggested as suggestions only. Receivers of ministry are to obey Scripture, but not necessarily follow what another human advises for application.

It takes humility to receive and follow instruction from a fellow believer. The Pharisees were too proud to learn. They already considered themselves experts and were not open to correction or change. They defended their own righteousness to the point of persecuting and crucifying Jesus. Pride prevents learning and growing.

Believers learn biblical principles by doing them. Just learning facts in the head or enjoying insight will not accomplish much unless there is action. Therefore, believers need to encourage one another to put into active practice what they are learning. As believers learn to look to Jesus, they can trust Him to perform the inner work. Jesus does the major work of transformation, while the believer cooperates and yields by working out whatever Jesus is working within (Philippians 2:12,13).

All personal care in the Body of Christ begins at the foot of the Cross. The one who ministers understands his own flesh and his own need to depend on the Lord. Although he cannot condone sin, he will be compassionate as he attempts to bring another person to the place of repentance, forgiveness, and faith.

> Brethren, if a man be overtaken in a fault, ye which are spiritual, restore such an one in the spirit of meekness; considering thyself, lest thou also be tempted. Bear ye one another's burdens, and so fulfil the law of Christ (Galatians 6:1-2).

One who minister's by grace through faith looks beyond the sin to the pain and the expression of the flesh trying to meet its own needs. He sees a person who needs mercy, but he also knows that biblical change comes only through repentance and forgiveness, assisted by instruction and encouragement.

12

Caring for Souls through Conversation

God calls and prepares all Christians to be vessels of His love and care. While the care of souls involves much more than speaking and listening, some individuals are particularly called and gifted to give biblical counsel to those who are experiencing problems of living. God teaches them in His Word and His ways so that they, in turn, may instruct and encourage others to know and follow God. Their faith in the sufficiency of God is imperative as they attempt to help people move towards wholeness, look to God for guidance and strength, grow in faith, and walk in the Spirit.

And such trust have we through Christ to God-ward: Not that we are sufficient of ourselves to think any thing as of ourselves; but our sufficiency is of God; Who also hath made us able ministers of the new testament; not of the letter, but of the spirit: for the letter killeth, but the spirit giveth life (2 Corinthians 3:4-6).

The one who ministers God's Word and wisdom is responsible to maintain his own walk with the Lord so that he will think, speak, act, and love more according to the life of the Lord Jesus within him than according to his own fleshly nature. On the one hand, he is to be a living example of Christ's life and to follow Paul's admonition to Timothy to "be thou an example of the believers, in word, in conversation, in charity, in spirit, in faith, in purity" (I Timothy 4:12). On the other hand, he must not deceive himself into thinking that he is beyond temptation or that he is in any way superior to the individual in need. Meekness and dependence on the Lord are essential because of the temptation to think anyone who ministers is able to help another person because of his own merit or abilities.

The care of souls through conversation may appear very ordinary. Two people meet. One has a problem and the other comes alongside to assist. They talk, but what they talk about is important in that it should be based on the Word of God. What happens depends first on the presence and activity of God in both believers. What happens also depends on the manner of care given by the person who comes alongside and the response of the person seeking help.

The care of souls is ministered in love. The primary love relationship is between God and His children. God's sovereign will and His grace far outweigh any human interaction. God must have preeminence as the only One who can transform a person into the image of Jesus. God is the Counselor, and His presence must be acknowledged throughout the conversation.

Trust in the LORD with all thine heart; and lean not unto thine own understanding. In all thy ways acknowledge him, and he shall direct thy paths.

Be not wise in thine own eyes: fear the LORD, and depart from evil. It shall be health to thy navel, and marrow to thy bones (Proverbs 3:5-8).

Next to the Lord, the most important participant is the person seeking help. He is the one whom the Lord graciously desires to mold into the image of Christ. Many people have approached psychological and biblical counseling as though the "counselor" and the process of counseling were the major elements of change. In psychological counseling the therapist is expected to bring about transformation through methods and techniques. But if change and growth are to occur in any kind of human interaction, a person's own desire, motivation, and willingness to change are key factors.

Even in the psychological realm researchers find that a person's motivation to change and assuming responsibility for behavior are far more important than the counselor or even the conversation. The *Handbook of Psychotherapy and Behavior Change* says that what the "counselee" brings into therapy has the greatest effect on the results.[1] Concerning secular counseling, Dr. Thomas Szasz contends:

> If there is any change in the "patient," it is, in the last analysis, brought about by the "patient" himself. Hence, it is false to say that the psychotherapist *treats* or is a therapist. It would be more accurate to say that the "patient" . . . treats himself.[2] (Emphasis his.)

In the care of souls, the most important person is the Creator. Next is the one who seeks help, but it is his response to God that contributes to his change. In psychological counseling, change occurs when an individual desires to change and takes responsibility to change. In biblical care, the person's desire, motivation, and willingness to take responsibility are also very important, but his relationship to God even surpasses what he himself brings to the situation. There is a combined effort in biblical change as believers are joined to Christ (Matthew 11:28-30) and abide in Christ.

Christians seeking biblical assistance need to recognize their active participation in making biblical changes through responding to God's enabling and God's will. They are not passive recipients, but active participants who can change as they respond in some of the following ways:

1. Biblical change can happen when an individual is willing to see his problem in the light of Scripture and seek biblical solutions. A person who will benefit from biblical assistance needs to be willing to see the spiritual basis of problems of living. He must be willing to look below the surface of the problem to what the Lord wants to change. In addition, he must be willing to seek spiritual solutions, to put off the old ways of thinking, feeling, and behaving, and to put on the ways of God as revealed in the Bible.

The Bible deals with all essential aspects of living, is a guide for righteous living, and presents reasons underlying wrong living. Problems that surface in thinking and behaving actually involve the spiritual realm. When an individual does not trust God, he has a spiritual problem that will affect much of his thinking and behaving. Fear, anxiety, pride, lust, self-centeredness, unforgiveness, rebellion, resentment, or bitterness often lurk beneath external problems. A person needs to be willing to see his problems as spiritual ones for which there are spiritual solutions. He can then come into a deeper relationship with the Lord as he involves God in the solutions. But if he sees his problems as psychological, he may rely on human help and self-effort.

2. Biblical change can happen when an individual chooses to change through God's love. Believers generally know more about God's will than they obey. But, as they move from their own ways (self-love) to God's ways (through His mercy and truth), they will be able both to know and to do. As individuals by God's grace desire to obey Him, they will find that He also gives grace to enable them to change and grow.

People vary in their reaction to change. Some individuals say they want to change, but they don't want to put forth any effort to do so. They want some external force to change them or to change their circumstances. Others are openly unwilling to change, and some are even unwilling to admit their resistance to changing. They want to avoid changing at any cost.

Psychological counselors have written about the paradox of people who come into counseling to change and then proceed to do all they can to resist changing. One psychiatrist contends that they seek counseling just to "go through the motions of changing while confirming that they have no real intention of ever really doing so."[3] Then there are those who believe they are being forced to change. Such people may do all they can to resist change and to prove that counseling is a waste of time.

In biblically caring for souls, love is the primary motivation for change. As a person learns about, believes, and experiences the love, patience, kindness, and gentleness of God, he will have a greater desire to love God through new thoughts and actions. Some Christians have difficulty believing God loves them. Often they are looking in the wrong direction—at themselves rather than at God. When a person looks at himself, he may not see how God can love him, but that is the wonder and greatness of God's love. One who believes God's love and responds in trust and obedience will receive instruction and will greatly benefit from godly counsel.

A believer who is well-grounded in God's love may only need direction as to how best to handle a situation. He will be willing to bear pain for the sake of another. He will forgive, forbear, exercise patience, and love in the most difficult circumstances. Nevertheless, even those who are well-related to God in love may need help and support of a fellow believer while going through difficult trials. Such people, as they receive and respond to God's love through trials, become vessels of blessing to others, and they glorify God.

3. *Biblical change can happen when an individual is willing to be responsible for thinking, feeling, and acting within the context of God's mercy and truth.* Many people resist taking responsibility for their thinking, feeling, and acting. Either they say they cannot help what they think, feel, and do, or they blame circumstances or other people. For some, this resistance occurs because they fear criticism. They need to be encouraged and motivated, within the context of God's mercy and truth, to accept responsibility for their desires, attitudes, thoughts, words, or deeds. Otherwise biblical change may not occur.

When people pay for professional counseling, they naturally expect the therapist to be responsible for the outcome. Because of the professional psychotherapist's training, degrees and licenses, his "magic wand" of theories, and his grab bag of specialized techniques, the person paying for the counseling easily supposes that the therapist does the work. After all, isn't that what he's paid for? Because psychotherapists charge a fee, they are forced to accept responsibility for changing their clients.

The biblical care of souls should not have this problem. The responsibility is shared with each believer being responsible to the Lord. The one giving care is responsible to minister mercy and truth as he assists a fellow believer to find help from God and His Word. He may also encourage, listen, teach, exhort, explain, and persuade his fellow believer to trust and obey. One believer comes along to help bear another's burdens so that the other person will be able to bear his own burdens in the Lord (Galatians 6:5).

The recipient of godly counsel changes, but not through the efforts of the care giver or through independent self-effort, but rather by abiding in Christ and thereby becoming like Jesus in thinking, feeling, and acting. Change that comes from abiding in Christ takes many forms. For one person, it may be choosing to hold a certain truth about God in the mind (Psalms 119:15); or for another, it may be choosing a different attitude (Ephesians 4:2). Whatever the choice, each time a person trusts Christ and obeys by His enabling presence, he changes and grows. Those who rely solely on self-effort, without involving God, may experience only superficial change.

Applying Biblical Principles of Responsibility

People may seek help to change other people instead of themselves. This is especially true regarding married couples. Each partner hopes the other one will change. Yet, if the attention can be removed from what the other person should do or away from negative circumstances, each partner can begin to trust and obey the Lord regarding personal change. In caring for souls, it may be necessary to discuss responsibility and change. Questions, such as the following may be helpful: Are you willing to change even if the other person (such as spouse, boss, or friend) or circumstances do not change? This question discourages a person from blaming others and encourages him to accept responsibility for his own attitudes, thoughts, words, and actions, even if he has been terribly wronged by others.

People may attempt to exonerate themselves from accountability by blaming others. But, those who blame others actually prevent themselves from learning and growing. Adults who blame their present problems on how they were treated by their parents continue as children. However, when they take responsibility for their own attitudes, thoughts, words, and actions, they will change and grow. When, by God's mercy and grace, people see their own failings, confess their own sins and repent, they will be ready to forgive others as they have been forgiven by God. They will grow when they choose to forgive their parents in the grace and power of

Christ. They will grow even more when they confront
and confess their own sins against their parents.

A person cannot easily move ahead in responsible
choices if he is blaming others for his problems. Nor can
a person receive forgiveness and cleansing if he is blaming someone else instead of confessing, repenting, and
choosing to change by God's grace. Much encouragement may be needed to move a person away from blaming towards taking responsibility. It is sometimes
helpful to ask, "What can *you* do to change the situation
(or relationship)?"

Blame began in the Garden and has continued
throughout the generations. When Cain's sacrifice was
unacceptable to God, he blamed Abel in his heart rather
than taking responsibility for his own choice of sacrifice.
The Israelites blamed Moses and God for the discom-
forts of forty years in the wilderness rather than obeying God and entering the Promised Land. Joseph could
have spent all his time and emotional energy blaming
his brothers for his troubles and ended up a bitter,
hostile old man. Instead, he trusted God, took responsibility for his own actions, and forgave his brothers.
David could have blamed Bathsheba for enticing him,
but instead he took responsibility for his sin, confessed,
and received the forgiveness and mercy of God.

Often a person enmeshed in self-pity sees himself as
a victim rather than a sinner. The so-called victim may
honestly believe that he cannot help what he does and
may think that he is "good" because he is doing the best
he can in spite of his hurt and fear. It's the ultimate
blame game with the weapons of hurt and fear. The
saddest aspect of the victim role is that if one does not
recognize oneself as a sinner, one can never fully know
the love of God, who gave Himself as a Lamb to be
slain. Jesus came to save sinners, not victims.

Although blaming another person and playing the
role of victim postpones facing one's own responsibilities, such a person wraps coils of self-deception
around himself that will cause great harm. When he

blames other people or circumstances or sees himself more as a victim than a sinner, he remains in his sins and does not grow in God's love. But, when a person faces and admits his sin and separation from God, he receives the forgiveness and restoration God makes available through Jesus. Proverbs 28:13 says, "He that covereth his sins shall not prosper: but whoso confesseth and forsaketh them shall have mercy."

Jesus gives Christians opportunities and abilities to be victors instead of victims, even in the worst circumstances. The person who has habitually played the hurt-victim role may not know Christ and need evangelizing. If one is a Christian, he needs to live by his new life in Christ. By following principles found in such Scriptures as Romans 12:14-21, Ephesians 4:22-24, 31-32, and 1 Peter 2:20-24, Christians can respond to wrongdoing in the same manner as Jesus.

The Lord continues to conform every believer into the image of Christ. Every person needs a good deal of transformation, and God allows people and circumstances to come into each believer's life to effect the change. The one who is always looking for change outside himself misses opportunities to grow. One who waits for others or surroundings to change may wait a lifetime. But, when a believer looks at Jesus and then at himself in the context of God's love, he is encouraged to become more like Him.

There is great temptation for one who ministers the Word to another to take more responsibility for the other than he should. But those who minister the care of souls must not violate the responsibilities and choices God gives each person. Every problem in a person's life is a point of choice. Every situation is an opportunity to trust and obey God. As a Christian chooses to submit to God and chooses to act according to the power of the Holy Spirit living within him, the Lord will accomplish the change. The one who draws alongside to help needs to follow the spiritual principles of Scripture. Where there is a misunderstanding or lack of knowledge, he will need to instruct. Where there is weakness of will, he will need to encourage. Where there is lack of trust, the one who gives care will need to love in mercy and truth. Where there is willingness to trust and obey God, he may only need to point the way. When each person aligns his will with God's will, transformation will occur (Romans 12:1,2).

As those seeking help for problems of living see the spiritual nature of their problems, not only through godly conversation, but through drawing nearer to God, they will be ready to cooperate with God as He brings the transformation. As they see God's possibilities for change, they will desire to change. As they come to know God better, their eyes are opened to what God desires to do in their lives. As they believe in God's available power, they will have both the desire and ability to change. An encounter with the living Lord Jesus, not only at salvation, but repeatedly and continuously throughout life, is the means for spiritual change and growth that affects all other aspects of living.

Guidelines for Pairing People in Mutual Care

Aside from pastoral care, women should minister to women, men should minister to men, and couples should minister to couples. A woman can more easily relate to the problems of being a woman than a man can, and vice versa. In addition, a woman can directly provide physical comfort to another woman. Because we use the Bible as the guide for all spiritual ministry, we attempt to follow those principles set forth in Scripture.

> The aged women likewise, that they be in behaviour as becometh holiness, not false accusers, not given to much wine, teachers of good things; That they may teach the young women to be sober, to love their husbands, to love their children, To be discreet, chaste, keepers at home, good, obedient to their own husbands, that the word of God be not blasphemed (Titus 2:3-5).

> But I suffer not a woman to teach, nor to usurp authority over the man but to be in silence (1 Timothy 2:12).

Furthermore, the examples in Scripture generally indicate that men advised men.

Much psychotherapeutic theory and practice have been developed by men, even though the majority of people seeking help are women. Lack of understanding by men has led to theories that attribute masochistic and other tendencies to women.[4] Many contemporary female writers are charging male psychotherapists with inflicting the stereotypes of society upon women, resulting in detrimental therapeutic outcomes.[5]

In addition to personal ministry being man to man and woman to woman, we encourage couples to minister to couples. The Bible calls the husband-wife relationship "one flesh." Rather than just being two individuals, a husband and wife together form a new unity. In couple-to-couple ministry, the elements of both members of the "one flesh" relationship are present. A woman can explain a woman's point of view, and a man can explain a man's for greater clarity and understanding when the couple needing help cannot seem to understand each other.

Pursue the Word

The conversation of biblical ministry must proceed from the Word and Spirit of God. To show the way of the Lord, the giver of Godly care must pursue the Word, pray for the Holy Spirit's guidance, and present the Lord's way as revealed by the Word and the Spirit. Jesus promised,

> It is the spirit that quickeneth; the flesh profiteth nothing: the words that I speak unto you, they are spirit, and they are life (John 6:63).

> But the Comforter, which is the Holy Ghost, whom the Father will send in my name, he shall teach

you all things, and bring all things to your remembrance, whatsoever I have said unto you (John 14:26).

As believers who are called to care for souls read and study the Word under the guidance of the Holy Spirit, they will be accumulating a treasury of life and truth from which to draw. As they seek to obey God's Word, the Spirit will bring forth truth. Furthermore, if they are both studying and obeying the Word, they will have both truth and wisdom to give fellow believers who are seeking the Lord's way.

Personal Bible study is vital preparation in caring for souls. As believers know and apply the Word in their own lives, they will be prepared to assist others in the way of the Lord. Out of the reservoir of living according to God's Word through the enabling of the Holy Spirit, believers will have God's mercy and truth to minister to others in need. They will be able to lead others into the pursuit of the Word for themselves.

Biblical ministry begins with the Word of God. This does not mean a quick and easy answer from the Bible, but sought-for, lived-through applications of Scripture. We cannot stress too strongly the importance of pursuing God's Word for ministering the care of souls. We encourage those who desire to help others to go to this source with confidence. No other way has such power for transformation.

Because of the importance of the Bible above all other sources of help, we do not attempt to present specific answers for specific problems in this book. While a specific system may shed some light and give some direction, it may also stand in the way of going directly to the Lord and His Word. If a method of care is spelled out, one may use that rather than diligently pursuing the Word and seeking the Lord's face. To say, for instance, that one must always approach a sinner in the same manner or with the same verse would not be biblical. Jesus, Himself, did not treat each person in an identical manner. He was direct and even harsh to the Pharisees, but He was gentle with the woman caught in adultery.

The stories of two different couples ravaged by the same sin may illustrate the need for dependence on God's Word and the Holy Spirit, rather than on a recipe book for counseling. Both stories involved adultery and the wives of both men sought help from the same older couple in the church. In the first story the one who ministered the care of souls met with the adulterous husband, relayed what he knew about the situation, and asked if he could help. The approach was gentle and caring. The adulterous husband was repentant and wanted guidance. The two couples then met over a period of weeks to encourage and support the decision to repent and to strengthen the marriage. Not only did God restore the marriage, but He has used this young couple to minister to others through the years that followed.

In the second story, the man caught in adultery came with his wife to the home of the same older couple. The wife was consumed with grief. This had not been the first breach of trust. The husband could not understand why his wife was still crying. After all, he was sorry and was ready to make things right again. In this instance, while the two women wept, consoled, and strengthened one another in the Lord, the same older man, who had ministered with all gentleness in the previous story, now ministered God's truth to this man with stern urgency. In fact, he was surprised at himself for his seeming harshness. Yet, he was speaking the truth in love, and the other man received it that way, even though an outsider may have thought he was too direct.

These opposite approaches would not have been effective if they had been reversed or if they had been exercised in the flesh. Yet, in both instances the marriage bonds were not only restored, but they were strengthened through the years that followed. Moreover, both couples grew in their relationship to the Lord.

Books utilizing a biblical approach to caring for souls can be helpful as long as they do not replace the guidance of the Holy Spirit and the direct use of Scripture. Books that give examples of how the Bible is used in ministering biblical care should demonstrate the effectiveness of using the Word. But a believer should not attempt to copy those examples specifically, for each ministry relationship is unique. Instead, there should be a spontaneous flow of the mercy and truth of God. Believers must go directly to the Word of God and to the Lord, who will open the Word and make application.

Pray for the Work of the Spirit

Throughout Scripture, the Lord encourages His people to seek His wisdom and His will through prayer. In fact, pursuit of the Word and prayer go together as one seeks the mind of God.

> My son, if thou wilt receive my words, and hide my commandments with thee; So that thou incline thine ear unto wisdom, and apply thine heart to understanding; Yea, if thou criest after knowledge, and liftest up thy voice for understanding; If thou seekest her as silver, and searchest for her as for hid treasures; Then shalt thou understand the fear of the LORD, and find the knowledge of God. For the LORD giveth wisdom: out of his mouth cometh knowledge and understanding (Proverbs 2:1-6).

The Lord accomplishes much of His gracious will for His children as they turn to Him to "obtain mercy, and find grace to help in time of need" (Hebrews 4:16).

Prior to ministering, those who care for souls will intercede for the person in need and for themselves to be clear channels of God's blessing, wisdom, truth, mercy, and grace. Much of what happens in biblical ministry is dependent upon what happens in prayer.

Asking, seeking, and knocking with persistence and a ready ear are the ways Jesus gave to find help for others as well as for oneself. Faithfulness in prayer is the mark of one who looks to God for change and growth and who continues to be sensitive to the working of the Spirit in one another's life.

In biblical ministry, conversation must be based upon communication with God. Some problems seem to persist in spite of careful instruction. Only the Lord can reveal the root of a problem or the way out for a particular person. One who ministers the care of souls is not just presenting the problem and asking God to do something; he is seeking to know how he might cooperate with God in bringing restoration, reconciliation, and renewal.

Those involved in mutual care may pray Paul's prayers for the early believers. Such prayers have great strength because they were inspired by God. Some of them may be found in Ephesians 1:17-19 and 3:16-19; Philippians 1:9-11; Colossians 1:9-12; and 2 Thessalonians 1:11-12. There are also many helpful books on prayer, but again the Bible must be the primary source for all a Christian does and says.

Spiritual ministry is spiritual warfare. A biblical care giver cannot win with fleshly or man-made weapons, for he is ministering in the midst of a spiritual battle between the God of glory and the forces of evil.

> For we wrestle not against flesh and blood, but against principalities, against powers, against the rulers of the darkness of this world, against spiritual wickedness in high places (Ephesians 6:12).

Believers who care for one another must maintain and wear their armor, practice using their shield, and become adept at using their sword, which is the Word of God. Their greatest and most significant activity occurs within their communication with God through reading the Word and praying.

Caring for the Whole Person

This chapter has focused on caring for souls through conversation. However, conversation alone may not be sufficient in many cases. Believers are called to minister mutual care to one another in many practical ways in addition to speaking and listening.

> And let us not be weary in well doing: for in due season we shall reap, if we faint not. As we have therefore opportunity, let us do good unto all men, especially unto them who are of the household of faith (Galatians 6:9,10).

As they care for one another, one may meet spiritual needs while another meets temporal needs, but all care of souls edifies the Body of Christ.

13

Cautions to Heed in Caring for Souls

Many warnings could be sounded about caring for souls. Most have to do with psychoheresy, distorted biblical doctrines, and the physical-nonphysical interface of human beings. As we have stated throughout this book, one of the greatest dangers in caring for souls is psychoheresy, which is the integration of secular psychological counseling theories and therapies with the Bible. Psychoheresy is also the intrusion of such theories into the preaching and practice of Christianity, especially when they contradict or compromise the Bible in terms of the nature of man, how he is to live, and how he changes. Psychoheresy can easily creep into caring for souls without the giver or receiver of care even noticing. Many Christians who hold popular psychological assumptions do not even know their origin. Worse yet, such notions and assumptions have been woven along with Scripture in sermons and Bible studies so much that Christians often mistakenly think such ideas are biblical.

A Christian's competency to minister is compromised to the degree that psychological notions have been embraced, because people will minister according to what they believe. The following is a brief list of some **unbiblical beliefs** that hinder biblical ministry in the Body of Christ. Believing the following **false assumptions** will hinder ministering God's grace:

1. The id, ego, and superego are actual parts of the human psyche.
2. A person's unconscious mind drives behavior more than his conscious mind chooses behavior.
3. Dreams are keys to understanding the unconscious and thus the person.
4. Present behavior is determined by unresolved conflicts from childhood.
5. Many people are in denial because they have repressed unpleasant memories into the unconscious.
6. Parents are to blame for most people's problems.
7. People need insight into their past to make significant changes in thoughts, attitudes and actions.
8. Children must successfully pass through their "psychosexual stages" of development or they will suffer from neurosis later on.
9. If I am to experience significant change, I must remember and re-experience painful incidents in my past.
10. The first five years of life determine what a person will be like when he grows up.
11. Everything that has ever happened to me is located in my unconscious mind.
12. People use unconscious defense mechanisms to cope with life.
13. People need to attribute worth to themselves.

14. People need positive self-regard.
15. Most problems are because of low self-esteem.
16. People need high self-esteem. They need to feel good about themselves.
17. God's main purpose is to meet believers' felt needs.
18. Christians can learn much about themselves through studying psychological theorists, such as Sigmund Freud, Carl Jung, Alfred Adler, Viktor Frankl, Carl Rogers, and Albert Ellis.
19. Christians need to be trained in psychology to really help people.
20. People need training in biblical counseling, because just knowing the Bible is not enough for helping people with serious problems.
21. The best counselor uses both psychology and the Bible.
22. Alcoholics Anonymous was started by Christians and is based on Christian principles.
23. Alcoholics Anonymous and other recovery groups are necessary for Christians to overcome addictions.
24. Learning about temperament types and tests can help Christians understand one another.
25. Professional psychologists and therapists are better at dealing with mental-emotional-behavioral problems than amateurs.
26. People must pay money to obtain the best help for mental-emotional-behavioral problems.
27. Paying for professional counseling effectively motivates people to improve.
28. A psychotherapist's training, credentials, and experience are all important ingredients for effectively helping others with problems of living.

We wonder how many Christians are able to read through the above list of false assumptions without thinking we are "throwing the baby out with the bath water." Documentation demonstrating that the above statements have no biblical or scientific support can be found in our previous books. Nevertheless such assumptions pervade the church and are being exported around the world through missionaries, who are supposed to be preaching the Gospel. As we look at the stranglehold psychoheresy has on the church, we wonder how many believers have become too psychologized themselves to be competent to minister *Sola Scriptura*.

Psychospiritual Healing

Probably the most difficult form of integration is that which is offered as religious or spiritual healing. The psychodynamics are hidden in religious words and prayers. There are many combinations, but one of the most popular forms of psychospiritual amalgamation is inner healing, which includes such psychological practices as scream therapy, rebirthing, resurrecting and reliving the past (including conception and nine months in the womb), guided imagery and visualization.

Leaping into the past, plunging into the unconscious, conjuring up false images, and dramatizing fantasies are the offerings of inner healing. One enticing practice of inner healing has "Jesus" enter a painful scene from the past. The inner healer helps the person recreate a memory by having "Jesus" do or say things that will make the person feel better. For instance, if a man's dad had neglected him when he was a boy, an inner healer may help him create a new "memory" of "Jesus" having played baseball with him when he was a boy. Through verbal encouragement, the inner healer would regress him back to his childhood and encourage him to visualize "Jesus" pitching the ball and praising him for hitting a home run. Some inner healers regress people back to the womb and lead them through so-called rebirthing by guided imagery and imagination. They should recognize the danger of unwittingly enhancing or engrafting memories through words or actions that mean one thing to the inner healer but may communicate something else to a highly vulnerable person.

People who remember sexual abuse and incest through inner healing are very likely "remembering" an illusion or distortion of reality through a destructive suggestion placed there by the inner healer, or created through a combination of stimuli, such as in a nightmare, or worse yet, demonic influence. Yet, those who participate in inner healing rarely doubt their newly discovered "memories." The certainty of the alleged memory has the mark of an hypnotically engrafted memory rather than of a distant reality. Who, then, can or will reveal the truth to them?

The Tragic Influence of Inner Healing

Many Christians have been influenced by best-selling authors and inner healers. Unfortunately those Christians believe such statements as this one:

> The realization of grace cannot be maintained in some people without an inner healing of the past. God's care cannot be felt without a deep, inner reprogramming of all the bad conditioning that has been put into them by parents and family and teachers and preachers and the church.[1]

Such Christian writers perpetrate false information and encourage erroneous beliefs. In spite of brain research to the contrary, they teach that the mind is like a computer and that there is an unconscious reservoir of hidden, powerful memories that highly influence a person's present thoughts, attitudes, and actions. They are convinced the memories they dredge up are accurate.

Inner healing practices of regressing into the past, fossicking about in the unconscious, conjuring up images, acting out fantasies and nightmares, and believing lies resemble the world of the occult, rather than the work of the Holy Spirit. An imaginary memory created under a highly suggestible, hypnotic-like state will only bring imaginary healing. It may also plunge people into living nightmares. People who unearth such "memories" end up with anger, resentment, unforgive-

ness, accusations, separation, and confusion. This is
just part of the picture of the damage wrought by those
who honestly believe they are helping people.

We were approached by a woman one day who was
seeking help for her daughter. Months earlier she had
enthusiastically exclaimed how she and her daughter
had attended an inner healing seminar and been
"healed" of all kinds of things they didn't even know
existed. Now she was desperate. Her daughter was
trying to deal with all the horror that had materialized
during inner healing.

People who are most vulnerable to inner healers are
those who are at a low point in their spiritual walk or
who are experiencing difficult circumstances. Some
inner healers entice through all kinds of direct and
implied promises for healing damaged emotions, healing roots in the past that prevent personal growth, and
enabling a person to have a closer walk with God.
Instead of being healed, however, there is a very strong
possibility that the recipients of inner healing are now
living on the basis of a lie from the pit of hell. Inner
healing is not based on truth. It is based on faulty
memory, guided imagery, fantasy, visualization, and
hypnotic-like suggestibility. While inner healers may
conjure up a "Jesus" figure and recite Bible verses, such
inner healing is not biblical. All religious approaches
that purport to heal memories and emotions or transform behavior and habits must be examined carefully in
the light of Scripture. The Bible plus rebirthing or the
Bible plus scream therapy or the Bible plus any other
psychological gimmick must be avoided by Christians.

Creating Memories

In addition to inner healers, there are "Christian
psychologists" and some who call themselves "biblical
counselors" who subscribe to the psychological idea that
people repress impulses and memories from conscious-
ness and that those impulses and memories continue to
act in powerful ways from an active, motivating uncon-

scious. Simply put, the scientifically unproved notion is that painful memories are pushed out of normal memory and packed into a powerful unconscious. Then those "forgotten" memories supposedly cause people to act in certain ways. This unproved Freudian-based idea suggests that if what is hidden in the unconscious can be exposed, people will know why they behave the way they do and then, with such self-knowledge, they will be able to change their thinking and behaving. If a "forgotten" memory of abuse is "remembered" in therapy, that serves as an explanation for one's present behavior. However, such theories contradict biblical doctrines on the nature of man and deny biblical doctrines of personal responsibility and sin.

Are "forgotten" memories newly "remembered" by individuals in therapy true memories? Are they really viable explanations for why people are the way they are and why they do what they do today? Most people, including Christians, would answer "yes," especially if they are involved in "Christian psychology" or listen to "Christian radio" or read the popular "Christian books." However, evidence reveals that memories are alterable and often unreliable. Moreover, there is no real evidence to prove Freud's theories of the unconscious or his theory of repression. Since there is no proof that what has been forgotten drives present behavior and feelings, it is counterproductive to search the past. Even if real memories of painful events are resurrected, the negative results may be worse than having forgotten.

Faith in theories of an unconscious filled with forgotten memories that cause present behavior has led to a special genre of psychologists who specialize in satanic ritual abuse. Numerous Christians are counseling according to those theories of unconscious repression and widespread traumatic amnesia. Countless Christians are newly "remembering" sexual and satanic ritual abuse in therapy and through reading books that encourage people to search for such memories.

Just as in inner healing, once people "remember" such horrible events, no amount of proof seems to dissuade them. Even when other family members say the abuse could not have happened and when pediatricians and gynecologists report that such abuse could not have occurred, the person "remembering" the abuse continues to believe those "memories." The result is not greater understanding about what actually happened. Instead, the recipients of such therapy seem to "need" perpetual therapy. Those accused of the abuse are further accused of denial (another Freudian defense mechanism). They are assumed to be guilty until proven innocent.

How Accurate Are Our Memories?

Some people would have us think that memory is like a tape recorder that records every event accurately and keeps it intact. But, research on memory has debunked that myth and raised many questions about common misconceptions regarding remembering and forgetting. For instance, how accurate are childhood memories? Does the vividness of the recall increase the validity of a memory? The Swiss psychologist Jean Piaget describes a clear memory from his own early childhood:

> I can still see, most clearly, the following scene, in which I believed until I was about fifteen. I was sitting in my pram, which my nurse was pushing in the Champs Elysées, when a man tried to kidnap me. I was held in by the strap fastened round me while my nurse bravely tried to stand between me and the thief. She received various scratches, and I can still see vaguely those on her face. Then a crowd gathered, a policeman with a short cloak and a white baton came up, and the man took to his heels. I can still see the whole scene, and can even place it near the tube station.

Notice the details of this memory. Nevertheless, Piaget then says his clear memory is of an event that never happened. Later, when he was about fifteen years old, his nurse confessed her wrong doing. Piaget says:

> She had made up the whole story, faking the scratches. I, therefore, must have heard, as a child, the account of this story, which my parents believed, and projected into the past in the form of a visual memory.[2]

Memories are created out of images, overheard conversations, dreams, suggestions, and imagination as well as out of actual events. They change over time. Even as we remember we tend to fill in the gaps. Each time a memory is recalled, it is also recreated with the emotions accompanying the recall and with the imagination which fills in the gaps. Remembering is not running an invisible tape recorder back to an event. It is pulling together bits and pieces of information that logically fit together. Nor can we depend on accuracy. Even immediate recall may be inaccurate simply because of an initial failure to perceive accurately. That is why people who testify about the same event may have completely different stories from one another.

Memories are also very malleable. They change even as we recall past events. However, with certain interferences, suggestions, or cues there is even a greater amount of creativity to the extent of creating false memories. In her book *Memory: Surprising New Insights into How We Remember and Why We Forget*, Elizabeth Loftus describes an experiment conducted with a series of slides showing the sequence of an automobile-pedestrian accident. She gives this information about what the subjects saw on the slides:

> A red auto was traveling along a side street toward an intersection at which there was a stop sign for half of the traffic and a yield sign for the remaining traffic. The slides showed the auto

turning right and knocking down a pedestrian who was crossing at the crosswalk.[3]

After the participants viewed the slides, an experimenter questioned them about what they had seen. Some were asked questions that included incorrect information. Others were asked questions which included correct information. Those who had been fed wrong information through the questions did poorly on recall and thought they had actually seen a slide with the information that had been suggested in the questions. Through this and other experiments, researchers have demonstrated that when false information is introduced, the memory can be altered.[4]

Hypnosis and Memory

When similar experiments have been conducted under hypnosis the results are even worse, since hypnotized people are even more susceptible to suggestion. Loftus says this research shows that "hypnosis does not reduce retrieval difficulties; it does not allow people to retrieve a true memory."[5] Many research studies show that what is remembered under hypnosis is just as likely to be false as true. Dr. Martin Orne, a well-known researcher of hypnosis says, "Hypnotic memory is clearly less accurate than normal waking recall."[6]

Dr. Bernard Diamond, professor of law and clinical professor of psychiatry, says research demonstrates that hypnotized people "graft onto their memories fantasies or suggestions deliberately or unwittingly communicated by the therapist" and that "after hypnosis the subject cannot differentiate between a true recollection and a fantasy or a suggested detail."[7] Loftus found that, after such experiments as described above, subjects continued to recall the false memory rather than what they initially saw.[8] Yet countless therapists, including Christians, use hypnosis in their search for hidden memories that supposedly will unlock secrets to explain present behavior.

Repressed Memories

While there is strong evidence that we do not remember everything totally accurately even under normal recall, there is also strong evidence that we do **not** tend to forget significant events in our lives. We may try to forget horrible experiences and we may reduce their impact, but the popular idea of a vast number of people having repressed memories of past abuse is just that—a popular idea. Research does not support that kind of amnesia to the extent that it is being promoted. Rather than being common, such amnesia is quite rare. Nevertheless, faith in repressed memories is widespread, because of books like *The Courage to Heal*, with such statements as: "If you don't remember your abuse you are not alone. Many women don't have memories, and some never get memories. This doesn't mean they weren't abused."[9]

While one cannot conduct experiments in which memories of abuse are implanted during the experiment, because of the resulting damage to the subjects, Loftus has conducted research on people (of wide age ranges) who were told by a relative that they were lost when they were five years old. According to Loftus, after the subjects were convinced they had been lost, they not only remembered the details told to them, but added even more details. The evidence of the power of suggestion to create the memory even without the use of hypnosis is amazing.[10]

Research on memory is important in terms of warning Christians seeking help for problems of living.[11] If any form of help or healing is regressive, in that it searches the memory for past events to explain present behavior, there is a strong possibility that false memories will be created. Once they are created, they are often stronger than true memories. This does not mean that all recall is false, but that there is a strong possibility that false memories will be created, especially if an inner healer or therapist is looking for something in the past to explain the present.

Right now there is great interest in recovering "forgotten" sexual abuse and even "satanic ritual abuse." The authors of *The Courage to Heal* supply a long list of symptoms, of which at least one or more would apply to nearly everyone.[12] Even though they have no research support, the authors are fully confident about their list of symptoms:

> If you are unable to remember any specific instances. . . but still have a feeling that something abusive happened to you, it probably did. . . If you think you were abused and your life shows the symptoms, then you were.[13]

Here is an example of one of the exercises suggested in *The Courage to Heal*:

> Take an event in your family history that you can never actually find out about. It could be your father's childhood or the circumstances in your mother's life that kept her from protecting you. Using all the details you do know, create your own story. Ground the experience or event in as much knowledge as you have and then let yourself imagine what actually might have happened.[14]

What kind of method is that for finding true memories and for discovering valid information about what truly happened during a person's childhood? Exercises such as these are ways to create false memories!

In her article, "Beware the Incest-Survivor Machine," social psychologist and researcher Dr. Carol Tavris says that authors of such books seem to be ignorant of scientific research in this field, that they "all rely on one another's work as supporting evidence for their own," and that they quote one another for further support. Tavris says:

> If one of them comes up with a concocted statistic—such as "more than half of all women are survivors of childhood sexual trauma"—the numbers

are traded like baseball cards, reprinted in every book and eventually enshrined as fact. Thus the cycle of misinformation, faulty statistics and unvalidated assertions maintains itself.[15]

Therapy that attempts to help clients recall forgotten memories may include hypnosis, but that is not necessary. There are other techniques that are being taught. One is systematically guiding the process of remembering. Questions are asked to "jog" the memory. However, rather than "jogging" a real memory, they may be supplying elements for creating new memories. Clients are encouraged to reconstruct events that are hazy and to visualize the location and other physical features. When the client begins to sense something the therapist will encourage the next bit of recall through questions that themselves may suggest incorrect information. In this creative endeavor there is a very strong possibility for suggestions to be made. While the purpose of such suggestions is to help the recall, they are often deceptive.

To understand the power of a false memory, think of something you know happened today. Now, what if a person tells you that what you remember did not happen? One person, who had seen a videotape of a woman with black hair and then received a suggestion under hypnosis that the woman was blond, said, "It's really strange because I still have the blond girl's face in my mind and it doesn't correspond to her [the one on the videotape]." The person continued, "It was really weird."[16]

Altered memories replace original memories. One does not have two competing memories (the old and the new). Even after seeing the evidence, the person continues to see the blond woman when recalling the memory of first seeing the videotape. Even external evidence may not convince some people that their memories have been enhanced through hypnosis or other forms of suggestion and guided recall.

Worse than feeling weird or losing inconsequential details of memory is the fact that many people are suffering great pain in the kind of therapy which attempts to dredge up old memories to explain present problems. They are now living with horrible memories of events that probably never happened. Those "memories" are now defining their lives. These people are now victims trying to recover from something that more than likely never happened. Rather than coming to the Cross of Christ, burdened with sin, countless people are going to therapy as victims. And rather than confronting personal sin and pointing a person to the Savior, such therapists are looking for sins that might have been committed against their clients and point people to their own selves. If believers in the Lord Jesus Christ would only take confidence in His Word, they would not get caught up in psychological counseling that attempts to resurrect the past in order to change the present.

Distorted Biblical Doctrines

Besides the intrusion of psychological theories into the church, there is also the problem of distorted biblical doctrines intruding into the care of souls. One distorted doctrine, propagated as truth and applied to those who suffer from problems of living, has to do with teachings about demons and deliverance. The practitioners of these activities are often sincere, but naive individuals, who truly desire to help others through some new "truth" or technique found in a book, workshop, or tape.

The distorted doctrine of demons reduces all human problems to demon activity and all solutions to deliverance. It is easy to identify the kind of person who embraces this distorted doctrine because he is forever labeling human problems and diseases as demonic. If one is fearful, he calls it a demon of fear; if one is depressed, it is a demon of depression (or a spirit of depression); if one has asthma it is a demon or spirit of asthma. The disease is always a demon, and the treatment is always deliverance.

One final warning concerns the potential damage that may be inflicted by the malpractice of deliverance. People who have been told by the purveyors of deliverance that they had demons and needed deliverance and who submit themselves to the process expect to be delivered. However, after various "deliverances," which include the usual "evidences" and activities of being delivered, no change occurs, leaving these individuals in a more desperate condition than before. One example involved a young woman who was depressed. She was encouraged to see a religious healer. After numerous repeated "deliverances" and "victories" she was just as depressed as ever. She concluded that she was infested with demons and that she was being destroyed from within. After "coming apart" she was admitted to a hospital, where it was determined that she had a biological problem related to the depression.

This one distorted doctrine of demons can cause real havoc in the care of souls and should be discouraged by any pastor encouraging the mutual care of believers. The distorted doctrine of demons can be the extremely devastating, because when people are desperate and deeply desire help they will reach out for almost anything available.

Misdiagnosis and Maltreatment

The intimate relationship between the body and the mind has led to misunderstanding and misdiagnosis during the entire history of psychotherapy. The history of biological disorders treated as psychological problems is an ugly skeleton in the therapeutic closet. Most psychotherapists would like to ignore or forget about their horrible means of treating physically ill people. At one time in this grim history there were physical diseases that were thought to be mental disorders because of the accompanying mental symptoms. Two examples are general paresis, caused by the spirochete of syphilis invading the brain, and pellagrous psychosis, caused by a dietary deficiency of nicotinic acid. In both cases numerous people who suffered from these diseases were labeled schizophrenic and treated accordingly. The following account is just one of many case histories involving misdiagnosis.

A twenty-two-year-old woman exhibited certain symptoms similar to those of schizophrenia. Rather than suggesting a comprehensive physical, the psychiatrist to whom she was referred diagnosed her condition as schizophrenic and treated her accordingly. However, it was later discovered that her depression and hallucinations were due to pellagrous psychosis, which had been brought on by a crash diet and near starvation conditions.

Sending a person to a mental hospital instead of treating the physical problem not only prevents possible cure, but adds even more horror to the agony of the disease itself. Can you imagine the number of people who have suffered from such physical diseases and were treated as insane, because the real problem was not known? Even Parkinson's disease was once considered a mental disorder and treated with psychotherapy.

This raises the whole problem of misdiagnosis and the tendency to refer people to psychotherapists. There have been and still are many individuals erroneously referred to psychotherapy who are really suffering from physical disorders. A number of people, whose "neurotic" and "psychotic" behavior has been caused by undiagnosed physical problems, have been treated by psychotherapy because the real cause was not recognized.

Another example of misdiagnosis, maltreatment, and the accompanying nightmare is found in neurosurgeon I. S. Cooper's book *The Victim Is Always the Same*.[17] One of the most pathetic parts of the book has to do with two little girls who had the rare disease dystonia, which is a neurological disease involving involuntary muscular movements mainly of the arms and legs. Before it was finally discovered that they were actually suffering from dystonia, the girls and their parents went through almost endless psychotherapeutic terror, all in the name of diagnosis, treatment, and help.

All the doctors and social workers involved thought only of psychological factors as they observed the overt symptoms, which consisted of strange movements while walking and odd, disconnected arm movements. These symptoms were regarded by the professionals as bizarre behavior. They concluded that the girls were emotionally disturbed and were symbolically acting out inner struggle and anxiety. They regarded the girls' parents as neurotic, distressed, and anxious. No one evidently stopped to consider that these parents were naturally concerned about their children and about the diagnoses that they were hearing.

The parents and the girls underwent weeks and months of individual psychotherapy and group therapy. One of the girls was even admitted to a psychiatric hospital. The more the symptoms persisted, the more the professionals accused the parents of not cooperating and resisting therapy. One child went through the agony of being interviewed in front of television cameras and also in front of other doctors. Worst of all, she was not allowed to see her parents, because the therapists thought the parents would ruin the therapy.

At last, quite by accident, one of the neurologists in the hospital happened to notice the child in passing and identified what she had—dystonia. Cooper reports that throughout this entire period of time the psychiatrists, psychologists, social workers, and group therapists demonstrated an astonishing amount of self-confidence in what they were doing. One might wonder about how much psychological damage they bestowed in the name of therapy.

Although this seems to be an isolated story, it is not at all unusual. In an article entitled "Dystonia: A Disorder Often Misdiagnosed as a Conversion Reaction," neurologists Ronald P. Lesser and Stanley Fahn state that, from the records of 84 patients who actually had dystonia, 37 had been originally diagnosed as mentally ill. They report, "These patients had received without benefit a variety of psychiatric therapies, including psychoanalysis for up to 2 years, psychoanalytic psychotherapy, behavioral therapy, hypnosis, and pharmacotherapy."[18]

The preceding stories are only examples of what can happen in this whole gray area of body/mind. Many persons have been given psychotherapeutic treatment without success and have even been wrongly hospitalized, because they were suffering from some physical disease or from inherited disorders like dystonia.

The tragedy of it all continues even today. Numerous physical diseases not only have been but still are being treated by psychotherapy with little or no success and at great loss to those unfortunate enough to fall into this trap of treatment.

Ministering to individuals with possible biological involvement can be an area of weakness for both the psychological counselor and the church. In some cases, recommending that a person have a physical examination may be in order. A care giver may also want to become familiar with prescription drugs and their side effects. However, those caring for souls should not recommend that a fellow believer stop or start taking medication. Such recommendations should only be made by a medical doctor. It is also unwise to make a person feel guilty about taking medication. Many people feel they are failures if they are regularly taking any kinds of pills. Yet substances, such as thyroid or insulin, help maintain a chemical or hormone balance in the body. Many people, however, with no apparent physiological malfunction are in ongoing bondage to tranquilizers that only dull the emotions without bringing any solutions. In either case, drug usage should be only under the direction of a physician.

We want to make it clear that we are neither recommending nor discouraging the use of medication. Our purpose is to bring more awareness in the realm of possible biological involvement and also to show that for too many years psychological counseling was used to treat biological diseases with little or no success, but always at great expense. In addition, we want to explode the myth that psychotherapy is the answer to extreme mental disorders. One who ministers according to Scripture has more to offer in guidance and wisdom to one who is suffering mental-emotional disturbances related to physical disorders than the psychological counselor has. Christians should minister the care of souls to those suffering from problems of living, and they should be available to assist those who are receiving medical treatment for biological diseases.

Misapplying the Medical Model

Because of the connection of psychotherapy to the medical field, especially through the specialty of psychiatry, people often equate psychological counseling with medicine. They ask, "If you go to a doctor when you're sick, what's wrong with seeing a psychologist?" That's because they confuse the use of medicine with the practice of psychotherapy. Individuals making such an error assume that the medical and the mental can be thought of and talked about in the same manner and with the same terms. This error consists of using the medical model to justify the use of psychotherapy. In the field of logic this is what is known as a false analogy.

In the medical model physical symptoms are caused by some pathogenic agent. For example, a fever may be caused by viruses; remove the pathogenic agent and you remove the symptom. Or, a person may have a broken leg; set the leg properly and the leg will heal. We have confidence in the medical model because it has worked well in treating many physical ailments. With the easy transfer of the model from medicine to psychotherapy, many people believe that mental problems can be thought of in the same way as physical problems.

Applying the medical model to psychotherapy and its underlying psychologies came from the relationship between psychiatry and medicine. Since psychiatrists are medical doctors and since psychiatry is a medical specialty, it seemed to follow that the medical model applied to all of psychiatry, just as it did to medicine. Furthermore, psychiatry is draped with such medical trimmings as offices in medical clinics, hospitalization of patients, diagnostic services, prescription drugs, and therapeutic treatment. The very word therapy implies medical treatment. Further expansion of applying the medical model to all psychotherapy was easy after that.

Medicine deals with the physical, biological aspects of a person; psychotherapy deals with the mind, emotions, and behavior. Whereas medical doctors attempt to heal the body, psychotherapists attempt to cure the mind and emotions. In spite of such differences, the medical model continues to be called upon to support psychotherapy.

Additionally, the medical model gives the idea that a person with social or mental problems is ill. With much sympathy people are labeled "mentally ill." Dr. Thomas Szasz explains it this way:

> If we now classify certain forms of personal conduct as illness, it is because most people believe that the best way to deal with them is by responding to them as if they were medical diseases.[19]

Psychotherapy deals with thoughts, emotions, and behavior, but not with the brain itself. It does not deal with the brain's biology, but with a person's mind and behavior. In medicine we understand what a diseased body is, but what is a parallel in psychotherapy? In psychotherapy mental illness does not mean brain disease. If brain disease were the case, the person would be a **medical** patient, not a **mental** patient.

Szasz very sharply refers to the "psychiatric impostor" who "supports a common, culturally shared desire to equate and confuse brain and mind, nerves and nervousness."[20] The assumption that medical illness and mental illness are alike is further dealt with by Szasz in his book *The Myth of Mental Illness*. He says:

> It is customary to define psychiatry as a medical specialty concerned with the study, diagnosis, and treatment of mental illnesses. This is a worthless and misleading definition. Mental illness is a myth.[21]

He continues:

> I have argued that, today, the notion of a person "having a mental illness" is scientifically crippling. It provides professional assent to a popular rationalization—namely, that problems in living experienced and expressed in terms of so-called psychiatric symptoms are basically similar to bodily diseases.[22]

Although one may result from the other, medical illness and mental illness are simply not the same. *Biological* and *psychological* are not synonymous. One has to do with the organic processes and the other with the thought and emotional life. The word *illness* after the word *mental* should have been rejected from the very beginning. Using the medical model in psychotherapy does not reveal truth. It merely disguises psychotherapy with the mask of medical terminology and ends up confusing everyone. Research psychiatrist Dr. E. Fuller Torrey says:

> . . . the medical model of human behavior, when carried to its logical conclusions, is both nonsensical and nonfunctional. It doesn't answer the questions which are asked of it, it doesn't provide good service, and it leads to a stream of absurdities worthy of a Roman circus.[23]

Using the medical model of human behavior and confusing *medical* with *mental* through false analogies could just as easily be used to justify support for ESP, past lives, UFOs, Eastern religions, and the occult. Transpersonal or religious psychologies are being supported through the same false analogy.

Applying medical terminology to mental life causes erroneous thinking and responding. The very word *medical* carries with it the suggested treatment, for if we are dealing with an illness, medical treatment is implied. Therefore, whenever someone suggests that you should believe in psychotherapy because you believe in medicine, remember that *medical* and *mental* are not the same. It is a false analogy and a false application of the medical model. Using false analogies and misapplying the medical model to the mind could even lead one to ask, "If you go to a medical doctor when you're sick, what's wrong with seeing a witch doctor?"

Psychology grew out of philosophy. Each theory behind each therapy provides a philosophy of life and a theology of man—why we are the way we are and how we change. Psychotherapy resembles religion more than it resembles medicine. After all the word *psychology* comes from two Greek words meaning the study of the soul. However, many psychotherapists and their advocates misuse the medical model to support psychotherapy. They continue to make this false analogy out of gross ignorance—to their own shame and to the detriment of others.

Conclusion

The warnings and information in this chapter are written to encourage believers to minister care to others in the Body of Christ. The believer may not yet have been confronted with the issues raised in this chapter. However, one who cares for souls will eventually have to deal with one or more of the areas mentioned. This chapter serves as a forewarning and provides information to which the care giver can turn when needed.

14

The Care of Souls
in
Your Church

Each body of believers that desires to encourage the care of souls should do so on the basis of scriptural guidelines and within the existing church structure. This section merely suggests ways to increase the care of souls in the local body. Some suggestions may not be practical in every church, but the framework may provide a starting place.

The care of souls should be under the authority of the local church body and accountable to its leadership. Each member should be in submission to the Lord, the leadership, and the Body of Christ. Just as pastors and elders prayerfully select Sunday School and Bible teachers, they can develop a roster of members, who are both doctrinally sound and full of compassion, able to minister to those experiencing problems of living.

Personal care of souls may also develop from a relationship of trust already established between a leader and member of a small group ministry in a church. Because of the heavy reliance on the Holy Spirit and because caring for souls is a function of the Body of Christ and an expression of the love of God, there should never be a fee charged for any such ministry. Ideally, all personal care should be a natural outflow of love and ministry in a fellowship of believers who know and love one another.

As with preaching and teaching, all personal care of souls (including encouraging, exhorting, giving counsel, or helping in practical matters) should: (1) be based on the doctrines of Scripture; (2) be rooted in Christ; (3) be dependent upon the Holy Spirit; (4) help one another to live the Christian life; (5) motivate one another to choose and do God's will; (6) nurture change, and growth; (7) be done in love. The same truths can be taught and "caught" from the pulpit, in the classroom, or during individual ministry. However, the personal care of souls touches specific needs and extends the mercy and truth of God. The source of mercy and truth is the same, but the gift, calling, and manner of ministering are personalized.

If church leaders plan to encourage the ministry of personal care through conversation, counsel, instruction, and helps, they may be faced with various questions and concerns. Through prayer and discussion they can determine needs in the local body. The following is merely a list of suggestions to consider.

Selecting Care Givers

Believers who have a saving knowledge of Jesus Christ can immediately begin to serve Him. However, the more believers are growing, the greater use they will be in the Body of Christ. The following list may be helpful in selecting those who might be used to minister godly conversation, counsel and instruction.

1. Loving the Lord with their entire beings. "The shalt love the Lord thy God with all thy heart, and with all thy soul, and with all thy mind" (Matthew 22:37).
2. Loving one another (Matthew 22:39).
3. Loving their Christian brothers and sisters as Christ loves. " This is my commandment, That ye love one another, as I have loved you" (John 15:12).
4. Living according to Christ's life and commandments (John 14:21).
5. Growing in the knowledge of the Lord (2 Peter 1:8).
6. Relying on the indwelling Holy Spirit (Romans 8).
7. Learning the Word and applying the Scriptures through faith and obedience (2 Timothy 3:16,17).
8. Using the Bible as the standard for all ministry (Hebrews 4:12).
9. Maintaining sound doctrine (Titus 1:9,2:1).
10. Praying for others and believing that God guides and directs His children and answers prayer (Ephesians 6:18).
11. Growing in the fruit of the Spirit, "love, joy, peace, longsuffering, gentleness, goodness, faith, meekness, temperance" (Galatians 5:22,23).
12. Being teachable and under submission to godly leaders in the Body of Christ (Hebrews 13:17).
13. Being consistent, dependable, discreet and responsible (Philippians 4:8,9).
14. Abiding in Christ to know when to exhort, encourage, teach, and show mercy (John 15:4-8).
15. Being mature in the faith— "those who by reason of use have their senses exercised to discern both good and evil" (Hebrews 5:14).
16 Being like the Bereans who used the Word of God to discern truth from error (Acts 17:10-12).
17. Being patient (1 Thessalonians 5:15; James 1:4).
18. Following his or her scriptural role in the home. If an individual is experiencing too many problems of his own, his ability to bear the burdens of others will be restricted (1 Timothy 3:2-5; Titus 1:5-9).

Educational training

Because the Bible is the primary source book for the care of souls, the ongoing Bible classes and sermons provide the basis for training. Those Bible classes and sermons which bring forth the application of God's Word in a person's life are the most useful for personal care, conversation, and instruction. If the pastor desires to offer any special training, he should only use those materials that are biblical. Quite often a church will turn to professional psychological counselors for training their members to care for one another, but we would not recommend that kind of training. If church leaders choose psychological training they will end up with something other than the biblical care of souls.

Matching People for Ministry

The pastor and elders may also decide to formulate guidelines on matching personal workers with those seeking help. Some believers thrive on ministering in very practical ways. The woman who coordinated our daughter's wedding was truly gifted in planning and preparing food as well as in organizing all the other details. As opportunities arise and members are encouraged to serve, people will discover areas of ministry for which the Lord has prepared and gifted them.

One area of ministry is that which comes through conversation. In this exercise of personal ministry, care needs to be taken regarding matching people with people as well as with ministry. To avoid temptation in the personal care of souls where people unburden themselves, we recommend that men minister to men, women minister to women, and couples minister to couples. Age variables also might be considered, since the one who ministers should have the maturity necessary to give godly counsel. While one does not have to have the same life experiences to minister to another, these can be beneficial. For instance, a widow, who has found Christ sufficient and has drawn close to him through having lost a spouse, may be able to minister more effectively than one who has not had the same experience. Also, being a parent gives one both experience and humility, which can be helpful in ministering to those having difficulty with their children. However, one does **not** have to have sinned in the same ways as the one to whom counsel may be given. All have sinned and come short of the glory of God. The way out is the same whether one has stolen a car, cheated on an exam, taken illegal drugs, or simply had a bad attitude about someone or something. The Gospel is the same for everyone. Conversion, if one is not yet saved, and ongoing confession, repentance, and renewed obedience for believers are the ways the Lord has provided for overcoming sinful attitudes, actions, and habits.

Ministry Load

Because mutual care in the Body of Christ is a shared ministry, no one ministering should be overwhelmed with too many people. Professional counselors have to fill their appointment calendar to generate a professional income. Therefore one of the doctrines of the professionals is this: Do not become emotionally involved with your clients. And no wonder! Can you imagine the emotional drain that would occur if a professional counselor became emotionally involved with forty different clients to the extent that he thought about them, prayed for them, became personal friends with them, aided them in practical matters, and felt concern for them beyond the appointment time and beyond the time spent writing up reports? However, Romans 12:10-15 tells Christians something different: Be involved.

> Be kindly affectioned one to another with brotherly love; in honour preferring one another; Not slothful in business; fervent in spirit; serving the Lord; Rejoicing in hope; patient in tribulation; continuing instant in prayer; Distributing to the necessity of saints; given to hospitality. Bless them

which persecute you: bless, and curse not. Rejoice with them that do rejoice, and weep with them that weep (Romans 12:10-15).

In the Body of Christ we are called to love one another. Love takes time, particularly when the person being loved is going through problems of living. Therefore, the care of souls needs to be spread out among the members so that it truly is mutual care. As many different members carry part of the burden, no one is overworked and each has time to drink from the Water of Life so that he can give Living Water to those who thirst.

Friendship

Some people would rather bare their soul to a complete stranger with whom they will not have social contact. They fear exposure to people they regularly see. They may feel as though the person who has listened to their secrets will socially relate to them according to those secrets. Also, they may feel exposed around the person in social situations, just because of the private nature of their former conversation. On the other hand, many people share their deepest thoughts and concerns with their closest friends and do not fear that their friends will treat them differently because of their confessions. Love that is expressed in a relationship of commitment, mercy, forgiveness, understanding, gentleness, and protection makes the difference. In the world of psychological and even biblical counseling, where the relationship is clinical and the "counselor" is in a position higher than the "counselee," later social contact may be feared. But if a godly friendship has developed during the care of souls and if a strong communication of mercy and truth has been established, then any further relationship continues in friendship and fellowship in the Body of Christ.

People who hold responsible positions in a local church may be reluctant to share spiritual shortcomings and failures of relationship with anyone in the same fellowship. And yet that is exactly what James exhorts believers to do: "Confess your faults one to another, and pray one for another, that ye may be healed. The effectual fervent prayer of a righteous man availeth much" (James 5:16). A believer who has honestly faced the depravity of his own flesh will not have a critical or self-righteous attitude. Rather, he will stand as a brother and friend to the one who is experiencing problems of living. Proverbs speaks of friendship as it relates to caring for one another:

> A friend loveth at all times, and a brother is born for adversity (Proverbs 17:17).

> Faithful are the wounds of a friend; but the kisses of an enemy are deceitful (Proverbs 27:6).

> Ointment and perfume rejoice the heart: so doth the sweetness of a man's friend by hearty counsel (Proverbs 27:9).

> Iron sharpeneth iron; so a man sharpeneth the countenance of his friend (Proverbs 27:17).

The care of souls and Christian friendship are quite similar. Both should follow Jesus' command to love one another as He loves us. Both call believers to bear one another's burdens and build up one another in the faith. Conversation in personal care and friendship should include listening in mercy and truth, responding with understanding, and speaking the mercy and truth that will best edify the other person.

The same things that can ruin friendship can ruin personal ministry: a superior attitude, self-righteousness, a know-it-all attitude, unforgiveness, possessiveness, bossiness, an authoritarian attitude, eagerness to give advice, disappointment with the other person, revealing secrets, and lack of acceptance.

Keeping confidences

Guidelines for keeping confidences also need to be established. One who ministers the care of souls will be very careful to keep confidences, but may occasionally need to share a concern with the pastor or church leader for the greatest benefit to the one who needs help. There are numerous admonitions in Scripture not to spread tales.

Coordinating Care

Most of the care of souls will function in large group and small group ministries and as believers fellowship with one another. However, there are times when special needs arise. The needs may be temporal, spiritual or both. One person may need assistance during a time of illness. Another may need help with housing or moving. Another may want to learn how be a better parent. Another may need godly counsel. Most of these needs may be met without anyone coordinating the care. However, having someone who has a list of helps and helpers available may be very useful. Many churches already have a coordinator for supplying meals to families when someone is ill. The coordinator for the care of souls could have a similar list of people who are gifted and available to serve in a variety of ways. People requesting assistance could be referred to the ministry coordinator. If the person requesting assistance is not familiar with the care of souls ministry, the coordinator could describe the ministry. If the person is requesting counsel, the coordinator should explain that the care of souls does not involve professional, psychological counseling or charge money for services. We recommend that such care be available to persons who are members of the congregation and to persons who do not have a church home, but who agree to attend worship and preaching services.

When an individual requests help, the coordinator may obtain such pertinent information as name, telephone number, times when the person can be reached, the general nature of the need, and other similar information that would be applicable. The coordinator would then locate a person in the congregation who is able to minister accordingly. From then on all arrangements could be made personally between the persons involved, unless another form of assistance is appropriate.

Principles of Care through Conversation

Ministering personal care through conversation, counsel, and instruction, involves the following:

1. Actively using the Bible and assisting persons to learn, know, and obey God through the enabling of the Holy Spirit. The Bible should be open and read aloud, especially by the person seeking assistance, because of what the Word of God accomplishes (Hebrews 4:12,13).

2. Remembering that the purpose of all ministry is spiritual growth as well as solving problems (Colossians 1:28).

3. Actively learning and growing in your own walk with the Lord (2 Timothy 2:15).

4. Remembering that ministry is more than conversation and being ready to serve and give in other ways along with the speaking and listening (James 2:15,16).

5. Cooperating with God's creative process of transforming believers through the renewing of the mind (Romans 12:1-2).

6. Listening to communicate love and concern and to understand the person and the nature of his problem (Proverbs 18:13).

7. Recognizing that each person and situation are fully known and understood by God, but only partially known and understood by the one who comes alongside (Jeremiah 17:9,10).

8. Trusting God to do the inner work (Philippians 2:13).

9. Not assuming that one knows the why's of another's sufferings (Job).

10. Loving and accepting one another as brothers and sisters in the Lord (John 15:12).
11. Edifying, which includes building up the person in the Lord, bolstering his faith and confidence in God, and enlarging his concept of the Lord (Ephesians 4:12,16,29).
12. Teaching, which includes correction and training as well as communicating God's ways (2 Timothy 3:16-4:4).
13. Giving counsel, instructing, or suggesting a plan of action or behavior according to biblical principles (Philippians 4:6-9).
14. Suggesting ways to apply Scripture to circumstances (2 Timothy 3:16-17).
15. Exercising patience (Ephesians 4:1-2).
16. Encouraging believers to cooperate with God in the change process (Philippians 2:12,13).
17. Being objective without losing the grace of compassion (Proverbs 3:3,4).
18. Comforting the person in pain; strengthening and giving hope with comfort to ease the grief or trouble of an individual, but watching out for the danger of too much sympathy; not commiserating with or pitying a person who is pining under his circumstances (2 Corinthians 1:4).
19. Seeing spiritual goals for individuals and helping them move towards those goals without imposing a form of legalism (Romans 8:1-4).
20. Maintaining an attitude of humility (1 Peter 5:5-6).
21. Praying with consistency and persistence (Ephesians 6:18).
22. Believing God's promises and His faithfulness to overcome the temptation of discouragement (1 Corinthians 10:13).
23. Giving all of the credit and glory to God for His work of transforming a believer (Hebrews13:20,21).

Self-Evaluation

Although the focus of all ministry is God and His Word and although careful attention is given to the person seeking help, one who ministers the care of souls must also attend to his own attitudes and actions. One way for a believer to prevent himself from becoming careless or lopsided in ministry is to seek God about the following questions:

1. Am I getting too involved in another person's problem, or am I seeing beyond the problem to God's ability?
2. Am I casting blame or bringing clarity and forgiveness?
3. Am I excusing sin or allowing the Holy Spirit to pinpoint what needs to be changed?
4. Am I offering the comfort of God or commiserating in pity?
5. Am I fearful of what a person might do (such as commit suicide), or do I balance caution with trust in God?
6. Am I following the guidance of God's Word and the Holy Spirit, or am I following the other person's emotions, flattery, or wrong expectations.
7. Am I either listening too much or talking too much?
8. Am I helping someone to become dependent on God or on me?
9. Am I exercising partiality or staying objective when there is conflict between two persons?
10. Am I relying on my own ideas and advice, or am I finding answers from God's Word?
11. Am I ministering in the attitude of humility or do I feel a bit superior to my fellow believer?
12. Am I developing a critical attitude toward a fellow believer?
13. How much responsibility am I taking for the other person's actions before, during, or after a care of souls conversation?
14. Am I becoming discouraged, or am I developing patience?

15. Am I blaming myself when there is little progress or congratulating myself when things are going well?
16. Am I becoming dogmatic and overbearing, or am I being gentle and kind?
17. Am I praying consistently for the person to whom I am ministering and for wisdom from the Lord?
18. Am I giving principles without suggestions for application?
19. Am I following biblical wisdom regarding scoffers, scorners, and fools (2 Peter 3:3; Proverbs 1:7; 9:8)?
20. Am I loving my fellow believer as Jesus loves me, in both mercy and truth (John 15:12)?

Times for Caring through Conversation

The duration and frequency of conversing for change will vary from person to person. The one ministering care will want to meet often enough and long enough to see change and growth or at least some problems resolved. Yet the relationship should not become one of ongoing dependency. A church may wish to establish guidelines to limit conversational care to a maximum period of time. However, the guidelines would have to be somewhat flexible.

The care of souls provides person-to-person listening and teaching, which believers need during certain periods of growth and especially during times of need. Within the caring and teaching environment of a body of believers, specific conversation regarding problems need not continue over extended periods of time. Because of all the other ministries in the church, particularly the worship, preaching and teaching, believers may need only an occasional conversation regarding specific problems. In the world, counseling goes on week after week until the client becomes wholly dependent upon the counselor. Long term "counseling" is not necessary in the Body of Christ, because ministry flows from so many different sources and because the dependency is on the Lord, not on receiving special care from a particular individual.

There are also times when it appears that a different person in the fellowship could minister better to a particular person. Certain people are drawn together as close friends. Others may care about one another in the Body of Christ but not be drawn together in the same closeness. Likewise in personal care, some people simply fit together better for ministry.

It is always a great blessing to see individuals grow closer to the Lord in relationship, trust, and obedience. However, there are times when individuals do not respond to personal care and move in other directions. When care givers see that a person is resistant to the ministry being given, they could pray about looking for a different member to minister to that person . However, some people seek help with no intention of changing. They remain scoffers, scorners and fools and waste the saints' valuable time (2 Peter 3:3; Proverbs 1:7; 9:8). There are also times when church discipline is necessary, in which case the elders should follow biblical principles.

The one who ministers care may express the kindness and mercy of God, point the way, and encourage. But the choice to follow the Lord belongs to the individual person. The care of souls is to guide believers towards abiding in Christ. It involves putting off the old ways and putting on new ones. It involves changing thinking and behavior, not just conversation. If there is resistance against trusting and obeying the Lord and an implied or stated threat that the one who ministers must not point out the truth, it is really best to discontinue. Such a decision cannot be made hastily, because the resistance may come from fear, rather than from rebellion, in which case more mercy and teaching about the Lord's grace would be in order, rather than termination of personal ministry.

If the personal care of godly conversation does not seem helpful, one should still be encouraged to continue in the worship, fellowship, and teaching in the body of believers. Persons who are not necessarily receptive to personal care may yet respond to teaching and preaching in large and small group settings. They should thus be encouraged to avail themselves of other groups, ministries, and personal relationships in the church.

Referrals Outside the Body

Almost every book written on counseling from a Christian perspective in the past twenty-five years recommends, at some point of difficulty, referring individuals to a community psychotherapist. Research does not support such referrals. For problems of living that can be dealt with through any form of talk therapy, the care of souls should be used.

Suicide

Threats of suicide are extremely frightening because of the possibility that the person will actually kill himself. No threat of suicide can be taken lightly or ignored, even though such threats may be manipulative devices or may not be carried out. Many people who contemplate suicide have lost hope for relief or change or are crying out for somebody to help them.

If a person is suicidal, more than one person needs to be alerted and involved. If any form of talk therapy (counseling) can help the suicidal individual, the church has more to give than a psychological counselor. Within a local church there should be enough people available to visit, phone, and pray for this person. The church has more time, availability, love, and help to give a suicidal individual than one lonely, fifty-minute-per-week psychotherapist. A church generally has enough members for around-the-clock availability when necessary. One minister cannot be available for so many hours, but when the responsibility is shared by the body there can be a strong supportive network. Furthermore, while some are ministering directly, others can be praying. Mercy and truth are both desperately needed by such a person. He also needs to understand the far-reaching consequences of committing murder.

Legalities

Most states regulate and license psychological counselors. But as long as no fees are charged and it is clear that what is being performed is not psychological counseling, the biblical care of souls will not be in violation of regulations concerning such secular practices. Biblical care of souls through conversation centers on Scripture, with the Bible open and read by both the giver and receiver of care. Biblical conversation and care are under the umbrella of pastoral care and are religious functions protected by the First Amendment of the Constitution. Even so, in our culture, lawsuits are common, and churches may wish to consider increasing insurance to cover any possibility of litigation.

Can the Care of Souls Help Everyone?

Measuring the results of the care of souls would be at least as subjective as the attempts to determine whether or not psychological counseling works. However, if we look at the most intensive form of discipleship (which is really what much of the care of souls is about) we do not find a 100 percent improvement rate. Even though Jesus ministered truth in mercy to His chosen twelve and led them into the deeper truths of the spiritual life and empowered them with authority over demons and diseases, there was one who was not transformed. Judas did not benefit or grow from the love and truth poured into him. He not only rejected the teachings, but he turned against the One who was about to die for his sins. In fact, Judas even committed suicide—after three years with Jesus. Can one say that Jesus' ministry was inadequate because Judas was not changed? Can one say that Judas's suicide was because of some failure in Jesus' ministry?

When Jesus explained the spiritual significance of the parable of the soils (Matthew 13:3-8), He revealed that, although the same seed is planted by the same sower in the same manner, the condition of the soil determined the fruit-bearing. Likewise in the care of souls, one may sow the same seed (truth) in the same manner (mercy), but the response of the person will vary. Some ground is very hard. While love may soften the soil, some people remain resistant. Others may quickly and eagerly try new ways of thinking and acting, but later discontinue fellowship and drift away from the church. Again, others may be entangled constantly in problems and barely grow into Christian maturity. Joy comes in seeing those who receive the seed bear much fruit.

Limiting the care of souls ministry to those who are or will become part of the fellowship will reduce doctrinal confusion. If a person is hearing one message at church and another one during personal care, he may be receiving more confusion than would be helpful. Personal care is most effective when it is part of the local church ministry.

Your Church

The foregoing organizational suggestions are just that: suggestions. A care of souls ministry must be designed by each individual fellowship in order to best serve that fellowship. The biblical care of souls is not to be an addition nailed onto the outside the church. Rather, such a ministry should be part of the very life of the church. Although it is spiritual, it should be the natural response of believers to one another. The Lord will lead in this endeavor as church members pray and seek His will through His Word and His Holy Spirit.

Although human beings are complex, the biblical care of souls is not as difficult as one might suppose. The basic elements are these: the Lord Himself along with His Word and His love; one who seeks help and wants a closer walk with God; and another who is applying the Word to his own life, who is walking consistently with the Lord, and who ministers the Lord's love through mercy and truth.

When Jesus asked Peter, "Lovest thou me?" He coupled his question with the command "Feed my sheep." He did not say, "Send my sheep over to another pasture." Jesus also said:

> I am come that they might have life, and that they might have it more abundantly. I am the good shepherd: the good shepherd giveth his life for the sheep (John 10:10-11).

The life Jesus gives comes through His Word, His Holy Spirit, and His people. The church is called, anointed, and empowered to give God's love and guidance to all who come with needs. What the Lord has provided through His Word, the Holy Spirit, and the church is adequate for all matters of life and conduct (2 Peter 1:3,4). Rather than running after the psychological way and amalgamating its divergent systems, the church needs to return to the biblical, spiritual way and to reestablish the care of souls ministry.

> Blessed is the man that walketh not in the counsel of the ungodly, nor standeth in the way of sinners, nor sitteth in the seat of the scornful. But his delight is in the law of the Lord; and in his law doth he meditate day and night. And he shall be like a tree planted by the rivers of water, that bringeth forth his fruit in his season; his leaf also shall not wither; and whatsoever he doeth shall prosper (Psalm 1:1-3).

15

Believers Competent to Minister the Care of Souls

The moment a person is born again by the power of God, "born, not of blood, nor of the will of the flesh, nor of the will of man, but of God" (John 1:13), Christ comes to live in him through the Holy Spirit. Because Christ is in him, he has all he needs to live the Christian life and minister God's grace to those around him. A babe in Christ is not yet ready for leadership and should not be given a leadership role before his life shows clear evidence of spiritual maturity (1 Timothy 3:6). Nevertheless, new believers are able to testify of God's grace, and they are able to serve one another. As they grow in their walk with the Lord and gain experience in the ways of the Lord, they become even more equipped to minister. Their competence to minister grows along with their spiritual growth.

239

It is grievous to hear people who have been Christians for many years say they cannot minister godly guidance and help to a fellow believer. The "best" they think they can offer suffering souls is encouragement to seek counseling, and by this they generally mean professional, psychological counseling, preferably conducted by a Christian. They have been warned not to give advice and not to get in over their heads. They are fearful to minister when they should be competent to minister. The simplicity that is in Christ Jesus has been made too complex for them. For too long the church has been adding so-called experts and their counseling systems to the Word of God and the work of the Holy Spirit. This addition has been a woeful impediment to the spiritual growth of individual believers and to their involvement in the edifying of the Body of Christ.

Competent or Incompetent?

Believers who are walking in fellowship with the Lord and are finding that God is faithful to His Word are competent to minister. However, some Christians are not competent because they have failed to trust God for all matters of life and conduct. They may not realize that they no longer trust God, but, if they hold any hope for psychological counseling or for biblical counseling that has embraced aspects of psychological therapies and their underlying psychologies, they may prove incompetent to minister biblically.

One reason many pastors find themselves incompetent to minister God's grace when members of their flock are experiencing problems is that they have been trained in just enough psychology to undermine their faith in God being able to accomplish His work without the help of psychological models and methods. They receive just enough instruction in pastoral counseling to feel adequate for minor problems of living, but inadequate for the serious ones. Because psychology and psychiatry have intruded into the nonphysical realm of life, many pastors have been hoodwinked into believing that psychologists can heal the mind and emotions while pastors can only minister to the spirit. But that's a false dichotomy. The mind, will, emotions are all within the parameters of the spiritual. Christ has come to live in those who are His, and He has made them new creatures. The most psychology can do is attempt to work with the old nature or the flesh. It has no jurisdiction in the new nature, "which after God is created in righteousness and true holiness" (Ephesians 4:24).

Pastors are not the only ones who have been undermined in their call to care for souls. Many believers are listening to Christian psychologists on the radio during the week, or they are reading self-help and other psychologically-oriented books written especially for the Christian market, or they have simply absorbed the notions and assumptions of a psychologized culture. Many Christians who hold popular psychological assumptions do not even know their origin. Worse yet, psychological theories have been woven along with Scripture in sermons and Bible studies so much that people mistakenly think these ideas are biblical.

Many who have confidence in God's Word for their own lives have been intimidated into thinking they are incompetent to minister. Yet, they are competent in Christ. They are competent through their own faithful walk with the Lord. They have the profound simplicity of Christ Jesus. They are probably not going to be the rich and famous or worldly wise, but they are called, chosen and competent in Him.

> For ye see your calling, brethren, how that not many wise men after the flesh, not many mighty, not many noble, are called: But God hath chosen the foolish things of the world to confound the wise; and God hath chosen the weak things of the world to confound the things which are mighty; And base things of the world, and things which are despised, hath God chosen, yea, and things

which are not, to bring to nought things that are: That no flesh should glory in his presence (1 Corinthians 1:26-29).

Paul refused to integrate the world's wisdom. He preached Christ and Him crucified.

And I, brethren, when I came to you, came not with excellency of speech or of wisdom, declaring unto you the testimony of God. For I determined not to know any thing among you, save Jesus Christ, and him crucified. And I was with you in weakness, and in fear, and in much trembling. And my speech and my preaching was not with enticing words of man's wisdom, but in demonstration of the Spirit and of power: That your faith should not stand in the wisdom of men, but in the power of God (1 Corinthians 2:1-5).

Do we think we are wiser than Paul because of the insights of Freud and others? Do we have more knowledge so that we can now integrate the ways of the world with the ways of God? Is God's Word less effective today than in the early centuries of Christianity? Did the church limp along all those years without 12-step groups and psychological insights?

The sooner Christians abandon the false assumptions of psychology, the sooner they will be competent to minister. We pray that God will encourage believers that they are competent to minister without the wisdom of the world. They are competent when they trust God and acknowledge Him at work in their lives.

So, which is it? Are believers competent to minister or are they incompetent? It all depends on what and in whom they are trusting as they minister. If they are trusting in God and His Word and Holy Spirit they are competent to minister God's grace. Each one may be only a small portion of God's answer to someone who is experiencing problems. But, that's the way God works, because He is supposed to get the glory instead of man.

There are still some people who believe God has work for them to do and grace to do it. Two young girls who have seen God's grace wrote the following in a letter:

> We have been very busy this year serving others for the Lord. We try to make sure that we worship Him first, then walk with His companionship, and lastly, do works for Him.
>
> We have a new ministry this year—a rubber stamp ministry. We make cards with rubber stamps that illustrate various Bible verses. We write to people who need encouragement, people who are sad, or just needing a reminder of a verse that would help them in their walk with God. Please pray the stamps will be a testimony and a blessing to people. . . .
>
> We also begin each day with a Prayer and Bible time. At this time we learn new Bible lessons from Mom (the Holy Spirit helps her to explain them really well). We then pray for people using our Scripture notebooks or rubber stamps. We then may write the person we prayed for a little note telling them what verse we prayed for them. We may not know what our prayers do for people on earth, but someday in heaven the people we prayed for will tell how God answered our prayers by helping them.

The girls live with their mother, whose husband died in a tragic accident somewhat over a year before this letter was written. The mother and daughters have been leaning on the Lord and trusting Him to use the tragedy for His purpose. Rather than looking for answers in psychology, they found a closer walk with the Lord. Rather than indulging in self-pity, they looked for opportunities to serve (1 Corinthians 3:9).

This dear widow and her daughters demonstrate that believers **are** competent to minister. May they inspire Christians to find ways to bless, encourage, and serve one another. Such quiet, simple ways to minister—like the widow's mite (Mark 12:42), which was far more valuable in God's eyes than the tithes of rich men.

Remember the game "hide the thimble"? As those who are hunting for the thimble search around the room, the person who hid the thimble gives such clues as "warmer," "colder," "you're getting hot," and "you're freezing." Sometimes that's a simple way to minister to one another. Exhort and entreat. Warn if they are walking the way of the world. Encourage and cheer them on as they are moving closer to the Lord. Help them turn around when they are moving away from the Lord.

Caring for Souls through Church Ministries

Believers are called to minister mutual care one to another in the Body of Christ. Such personal ministry, based on scriptural guidelines, should be happening within every church. Rather than sending Christians to outside counseling, each local fellowship should provide pastoral and mutual care. Since the care of souls is a function of the church, based on God's love and truth and dependent on God's Word and Holy Spirit, no fee should be charged for godly counsel. Additionally, the care of souls is more than conversation. It is mutually serving one another wherever and whenever the need arises. Ideally, personal care for one another should be a natural outflow of love and ministry in a fellowship of believers who know and love one another. This personal care includes giving time and talents. Just being available to one another can be a great encouragement, especially during various difficulties. As Christians give to one another, serve one another, and love one another, they help each other mature in the faith, build up Christ's Body, and bring glory to God.

Whenever there is a need, it is extremely helpful when a pastor or elder can call upon a believer within the local fellowship to help. When the need concerns problems of living, a fellow believer can come alongside to minister God's grace so that the person is not sent to professional counselors outside the church, who might counsel according to philosophies and teachings not in agreement with the teachings of the fellowship. No section of Scripture instructs elders to send believers outside the church to find help for problems of living. Jesus called His disciples to minister according to His Word, and He sent His Holy Spirit to be the Counselor. While some may be gifted by the Lord for various aspects of personal ministry, each believer in whom the Lord dwells can minister personal care as the Lord gives opportunity.

The basic elements for transformation and growth already exist within a church where there is biblical love and sound scriptural teaching. The care of souls includes evangelizing, preaching, and teaching. The care of souls also includes personal care, which is actually an extension of those same ministries, but done on a more personal level. The personal care may be a word of witness to bring a friend to Christ, an explanation or exposition of Scripture, a reminder or encouragement, an act of mercy or kindness, a word of exhortation, or practical help, such as giving rides to church, caring for a sick person, visiting shut-ins, taking care of children, or doing whatever good is at hand to do. It is coming alongside in mercy and truth to minister the grace of God in time of need. God's grace may come through what may appear to be an insignificant act of kindness or through a sharp rebuke motivated by love.

Just as the Holy Spirit and the Word of God work together to build up the Body of Christ through teaching and preaching, the Holy Spirit and Word of God work together to build up individual members through the mutual care of souls. Caring for souls involves preaching and teaching the Word, fellowship, and prayer. Believers are called to love one another through truly caring about one another and becoming involved, not as busy bodies, but as family members, who are willing to serve one another. Personal care is an individualized extension of group ministries in the church.

Caring for souls becomes personal through giving time and helping one another in practical ways. If biblical counsel is to be given, it is not separated from other needs. There are times when words need to be accompanied by actions. It is not enough to say, "Be ye warmed and filled," if the person has no means to be warm or filled on his own. God has given His Word, but He also gives us our daily bread. Words and actions both speak of the goodness, generosity, and love of God.

Many people feel inadequate to minister if they have not completed a special course or earned a seminary degree. Yet, they are often the very ones who are best equipped to minister. They are especially equipped as they are growing in the Lord and obeying His Word. They are ready to minister as they live humbly according to what God has taught them and as they walk by faith. These are the believers who have been equipped by the Lord Himself to minister the care of souls. Many Christians have learned to live their lives according to the love of God and the truth of His Word. They are more than competent to minister in the Body of Christ.

Care of Souls When Believers Gather Together

The church cares for souls as it meets together for worship and for preaching and teaching the Word for evangelism, instruction in how to live, and the edification of the entire Body. One cannot over-emphasize the importance of preaching and teaching. Corporate worship and preaching the Word are essential. Through this broad ministry many lives are touched. Even when many believers are gathered together to hear preaching, the Holy Spirit works individually in each person. Preaching may look foolish to the world, but God has ordained preaching as a means for the Gospel to be communicated and for believers to be instructed. If the teaching and preaching are biblically sound and communicated in love, and if the believers are responding, then many in the congregation will be growing spiritually and meeting life's challenges. The pulpit supplies opportunities to present valuable lessons from the Word that apply to daily living. Scripture, properly taught, has life-transforming effects. As a pastor brings forth God's love and applies His Word, lives are changed. Preaching and teaching God's Word equip believers to minister mutual care to one another.

Besides meeting together for corporate worship, Christians may also meet in smaller groups for Bible instruction and also for ministry at a more personal level. These groups should be under the authority and teaching ministry of the local church. When believers gather together in small groups, they have opportunities to get to know one another and therefore to minister mutual care. Love can be given in a general way in a large group setting, but when a member of Christ's Body is facing difficult trials and temptations or working on important decisions, he may benefit from the consistent, regular, through-the-week involvement a small group can provide.

As small groups follow the forms presented in Scripture, rather than recycled humanistic systems, they can participate in Jesus' commandment to "love one another as I have loved you." A group leader would do well to search Scripture and seek the Lord in leading the group, rather than learn techniques that might reduce the whole process to a sterile methodology or to an experience-driven, encounter group. The small group should be the visible expression of the Body of Christ and therefore operate according to His character and Word. Praying for one another in the group leads to concern and help as members become sensitive to one another's needs.

Effective personal care of souls can occur in Christ-centered, small groups. Many problems and potential problems of living faced by members of a local church can be alleviated by preaching God's Word and encouraging each other as persons being formed by Christ, bearing one another's burdens, and praying. Then, when small groups meet in homes, people get to know one another better and begin to share and worship together on a more intimate basis. A fellowship that loves God and neighbor as self will be the best antidote for trials, troubles, and tribulations of life. Human love has always been a beneficial balm. But greater than this is the love of God expressed and received in a fellowship of believers.

A Talking "Cure" or Speaking the Truth in Love?

The church has permitted the "cure" of minds and emotions (psychotherapy) to replace the biblical care of souls without sufficient justification. It has adopted and dispensed psychotherapeutic theories, techniques, and terminology in its attempt to minister to those suffering from problems of living. It has embraced the talking "cure" at the expense of the biblical care of souls. Moreover, many who claim to be biblical counselors merely reflect the ways of the world. (We wrote *Against Biblical Counseling: For the Bible* for that very reason.)

We have a living God, the source of all life and healing. We have His living, enduring, abiding Word (1 Peter 1:23-25). His Word contains the balm of Gilead for troubled souls. His Word ministers truth to the mind, direction and encouragement to the will, and grace for the emotions.

While believers may find great help speaking and listening to one another, such conversation should be biblically grounded rather than psychologically tainted. One should also be ready to give more than conversation. Believers have the Word of God and the mind of Christ. When they speak to one another, their speech is to be truth spoken in love. As they listen to one another, they are to listen for truth, God's truth, which sets one free, instead of worldly opinions.

If you are one who needs assistance, look for someone in your local church who can minister to you. For example, if you are suffering mentally and emotionally, look for someone who is mature in the faith and is walking with God the way you desire to walk. Ask that person to come alongside and minister God's Word and pray. Whatever your needs, find someone or ask your pastor or elders to find a person to assist you in your walk with the Lord.

Every Believer Is Competent to Care for Souls!

The Lord has given His Body all they need to minister. He will use young believers, mature believers, leaders, and followers who will trust in Christ's sufficiency and the completeness of God's Word. They will minister under the anointing of the Holy Spirit and rely on His blessed Word. They will operate as a priesthood of all believers and minister God's love, grace, mercy, faithfulness, and wisdom to one another. They will voluntarily give time, love, and whatever else is needful to help one another through difficult circumstances. They will care for one another and diligently pray for one another. Some are already doing all these things and they are seeing fruit and being blessed.

The biblical care of souls involves more than just biblical conversation. It involves biblically caring for the whole person through the mutual participation of all members of the Body of Christ. The biblical care of souls first and foremost consists of caring for a person's eternal destiny, which encompasses salvation and sanctification. Though the biblical care of souls is a high calling, it is a common calling to minister to the inner and outer person, utilizing the whole counsel of God by grace through faith with hope and love. Caring for souls includes godly conversation ministered in mercy and truth with wisdom. Under the leadership of the local church, believers are competent to minister mutual care to the glory of God.

God asks in His Word, "Whom shall I send, and who will go for us?" This is a call to serve and minister.

May every believer answer, "Here am I; send me."

Soli Deo Gloria!

End Notes

Chapter 1: *The Biblical Care of Souls in the Body of Christ*
1. Martin and Deidre Bobgan. *The Psychological Way / The Spiritual Way.* Minneapolis: Bethany Press, 1979.
2. Martin and Deidre Bobgan. *How to Counsel from Scripture.* Chicago: Moody Press, 1985.
3. John T. McNeill. *A History of the Cure of Souls.* New York: Harper & Row, 1951, p. vii.
4. *Ibid.*, p. vii.
5. See *Four Temperaments, Astrology & Personality Testing.* Martin and Deidre Bobgan. Santa Barbara, CA: EastGate Publishers, 1992.
6. Martin and Deidre Bobgan. *Against Biblical Counseling: For the Bible.* Santa Barbara, CA: EastGate Publishers, 1994, p. 11.

Chapter 2: *Getting Past the Obstacles to Caring for Souls*
1. Martin and Deidre Bobgan. *PsychoHeresy: The Psychological Seduction of Christianity.* Santa Barbara: EastGate Publishers, 1987.
2. Sutherland, P. and Poelstra, P. "Aspects of Integration." Paper presented at the meeting of the Western Association of Christians for Psychological Studies, Santa Barbara, CA, June 1976.
3. Truax and Mitchell quoted by Sol Garfield, "Psychotherapy Training and Outcome in Psychotherapy," BMA Audio Cassette #T-305. New York: Guilford, 1979.
4. Morris B. Parloff, "Psychotherapy and Research: An Anaclitic Depression," *Psychiatry* 43, November 1980, p. 288.
5. Jerome Frank, "Mental Health in a Fragmented Society: The Shattered Crystal Ball," American *Journal of Orthopsychiatry* 49, no. 3, July 1979, p. 406.
6. Hans H. Strupp and Suzanne W. Hadley, "Specific vs Nonspecific Factors in Psychotherapy," *Archives of General Psychiatry* 36, September 1979, p. 1126.
7. Bobgan, *PsychoHeresy op. cit.*, Chap. 14.
8. Bernie Zilbergeld quoted by Don Stanley, "OK So Maybe You Don't Need to See a Therapist," *Sacramento Bee,* 24, May 1983, p. B-4.
9. Robyn M. Dawes. *House of Cards: Psychology and Psychotherapy Built on Myth.* New York: The Free Press, 1994, p. 52.
10. *Ibid.*, p. 55.
11. Jeffrey S. Berman and Nicholas C. Norton, "Does Professional Training Make a Therapist More Effective?" *Psychological Bulletin*, 98, 1985, pp. 401-407.

Chapter 4: *A High Calling; A Common Calling*
1. Martin Luther quoted in *New Dictionary of Theology.* Sinclair B. Ferguson et al, eds. Downers Grove: InterVarsity Press, 1988, p. 532.

Chapter 5: *Caring for Souls Inside and Out*
1. E. Brooks Holifield. *A History of Pastoral Care in America: From Salvation to Self-Realization.* Nashville: Abingdon Press, 1983, p. 27.
2. *Ibid.*, p. 23.
3. *Ibid.*, p. 65.
4. Martin Gross. *The Psychological Society.* New York: Randon House, 1978.
5. Thomas N. Smith, "The Perils of Puritanism," *Reformation & Revival*, Vol. 5, No. 2, Spring 1996, p. 95.

Chapter 8: *Living and Ministering by Faith*
1. Jerome Frank. *Persuasion and Healing.* New York: Schocken Books, 1961, 1974 ed., p. 325.
2. Thomas Szasz. *The Myth of Psychotherapy.* Garden City: Doubleday/Anchor press, 1978, p. 35.
3. Arthur K. Shapiro interview. Martin Gross. *The Psychological Society.* New York: Random House, 1978, p. 230.
4. Frank, *op. cit.*, p. 60.

Chapter 11: Ministering Mercy and Truth

1. Lori B. Andrews, "What People Don't Tell Therapists," *Psychology Today,* September 1982, p. 16.
2. Kenneth Woodward, "Lying All the Way to the Truth," *Psychology Today,* November 1982, p. 20.

Chapter 12: *Caring for Souls through Conversation*

1. Allen E. Bergin and Michael J. Lambert, "The Evaluation of Therapeutic Outcomes," in *Handbook of Psychotherapy and Behavior Change,* ed. Sol L. Garfield and Allen E. Bergin (New York: John Wiley & Sons, 1978), p. 180.
2. Thomas Szasz, *The Myth of Psychotherapy* (Garden City, N.Y.: Doubleday, Anchor, 1978), p. 190.
3. Eric Marcus, "The Use of Paradox," *Association for Humanistic Psychology Newsletter,* December 1982, p. 6.
4. "Shrinks Lobotomize ERA," *Mother Jones,* July 1980, p. 10.
5. Julia Sherman, "Psychotherapy with Women," BMA Audio Cassette, #T-330. (New York: Guilford, n.d.). Annette M. Brodsky and Rachel Hare-Mustin, *Women and Psychotherapy* (New York: Guilford, 1980).

Chapter 13: *Cautions to Heed in Caring for Souls*

1. David Seamands. *Healing for Damaged Emotions.* Wheaton: Victor Books, 1981, p. 85.
2. Jean Piaget, *Plays, Dreams and Imitation in Childhood* (New York: Norton, 1962).
3. Elizabeth Loftus. *Memory: Surprising New Insights into How We Remember and Why We Forget.* Reading, MA: Addison-Wesley Publishing Company, 1980, p. 46.
4. *Ibid.,* pp 46-47.
5. *Ibid.,* p. 48.
6. Martin Orne, *Psychology Today,* February 1984, p. 35.
7. Bernard L. Diamond, "Inherent Problems in the Use of Pretrial Hypnosis on a Prospective Witness," *California Law Review,* March 1980, p. 348.
8. Loftus, *op. cit.,* pp. 48-49.
9. Ellen Bass and Laura Davis. *The Courage to Heal.* San Francisco: HarperCollins, 1988, p. 81.
10. Elizabeth F. Loftus, "The Reality of Repressed Memories" an expanded version of her Psi Chi/Frederick Howell Leis Distinguished Lecture address at the American Psychological Association, Washington, DC, August, 1992.
11. For additional research information on false memories, contact the False Memory Foundation, 3508 Market Street, Philadelphia, PA 19104.
12. Carol Tavris, "Beware the Incest-Survivor Machine," *The New York Times Book Review,* January 3, 1993, p. 1.
13. Bass and Davis, *op. cit.,* pp. 21-22.
14. *Ibid.,* p. 154.
15. Tavris, *op. cit.*
16. Loftus, *op. cit.,* p. 48.
17. I. S. Cooper. *The Victim Is Always the Same.* New York: Harper and Row, 1973.
18. Ronald P. Lesser and Stanley Fahn, "Dystonia: A Disorder Often Misdiagnosed as a Conversion Reaction." *American Journal of Psychiatry,* Vol. 135, No. 3, March 1978, p. 350.
19. Thomas Szasz. *The Myth of Psychotherapy.* Garden City: Doubleday/Anchor Press, 1978, pp. 182-183.
20. *Ibid.,* p. 7.
21. Thomas Szasz. *The Myth of Mental Illness.* New York: Harper and Row, 1974), p. 262.
22. *Ibid.*
23. E. Fuller Torrey. *The Death of Psychiatry.* Radnor: Chilton Book Company, 1974, p. 24.

OTHER BOOKS FROM EASTGATE

PsychoHeresy: The Psychological Seduction of Christianity by Martin and Deidre Bobgan exposes the fallacies and failures of psychological counseling theories and therapies for one purpose: to call the Church back to curing souls by means of the Word of God and the work of the Holy Spirit rather than by man-made means and opinions. Besides revealing the anti-Christian biases, internal contradictions, and documented failures of secular psychotherapy, *PsychoHeresy* examines various amalgamations of secular psychologies with Christianity and explodes firmly entrenched myths that undergird those unholy unions.

Christian Psychology's War On God's Word: The Victimization Of The Believer by Jim Owen is about the sufficiency of Christ and about how "Christian" psychology undermines believers' reliance on the Lord. Owen demonstrates how "Christian" psychology pathologizes sin and contradicts biblical doctrines of man. He further shows that "Christian" psychology treats people more as victims needing psychological intervention than sinners needing to repent. Owen beckons believers to turn to the all-sufficient Christ and to trust fully in His ever-present provisions, the power of His indwelling Holy Spirit, and the sure guidance of the inerrant Word of God.

12 Steps to Destruction: Codependency/Recovery Heresies by the Bobgans provides information for Christians about codependency/recovery teachings, Alcoholics Anonymous, Twelve-Step groups, and addiction treatment programs. All are examined from a biblical, historical, and research perspective. The book urges believers to trust the sufficiency of Christ and the Word of God instead of Twelve Steps and codependency/recovery theories and therapies.

Four Temperaments, Astrology & Personality Testing by the Bobgans answers such questions as: Do the four temperaments give valid information? Are there biblically or scientifically established temperament or personality types? Are personality inventories and tests valid ways of finding out about people? How are the four temperaments, astrology, and personality testing connected? Personality types and tests are examined from a biblical, historical, and research basis.

Against Biblical Counseling: For the Bible by Martin and Deidre Bobgan is about the growing biblical counseling movement and urges Christians to return to biblically ordained ministries and mutual care in the Body of Christ. It is an analysis of what biblical counseling is, rather than what it pretends or even hopes to be. Its primary thrust is to call Christians back to the Bible and to biblically ordained ministries and mutual care in the Body of Christ, "For the perfecting of the saints, for the work of the ministry, for the edifying of the body of Christ" (Ephesians 4:12).